Thirteen keys to unlock your power

A guide to exponentially enhance your life

Tanu Vatsa Aggarwal

Life Empowerment Coach
ACC, International Coach Federation

First published in 2020 by
Independently published

ISBN: 979-86-69701-79-6

ABOUT THE AUTHOR

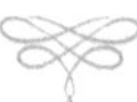

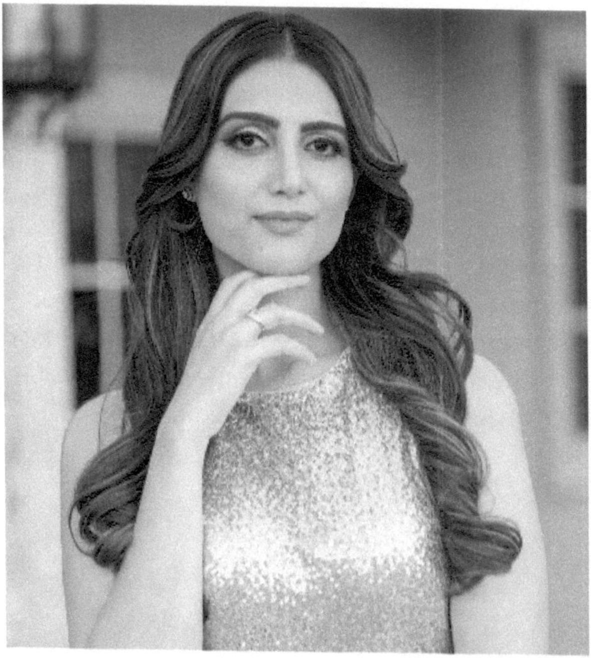

Tanu Vatsa Aggarwal is a practicing Life Empowerment Coach in Dallas, TX. She has been certified as an Associate Certified Coach by the International Coach Federation, USA. A highly acclaimed professional in her field, she has been featured in various television talk shows and magazines. With several hundred hours of coaching experience under her belt, she partners with her clients in a thought provoking and creative process that inspires them to maximize their personal and professional potential. She provides coaching services for a range of areas including personal development, relationships, lifestyle, business and career.

She is also a successful entrepreneur, and runs a business of luxury custom furniture – Opulent International, Inc. A philanthropist at heart, she supports various charities for disaster relief, animal care, support for cancer patients, rehabilitation for human trafficking and domestic abuse victims. The cause of women empowerment is very close to her heart. She provides pro-bono business coaching for women in underdeveloped countries of Afghanistan and Rwanda.

CONTENTS

INTRODUCTION

"Your only obligation in any lifetime is to be true to yourself." — Richard Bach, Illusions

Evolution is a powerful force and it equips all organisms with the power to not only survive but to thrive in their natural environments. Honey bees naturally know how to dance and communicate with others of their species. Spiders instinctively know how to spin webs. Some animals are born with the knowledge of migrating patterns. These instinctive traits are hardwired in our brains and in our default operating systems. Some of these instincts are primal, such as sucking response, grasping, crying, making noises, and facial expressions, whereas others are more complex, such as courtship behaviors.

We humans are no different. We already have what it takes to make our lives work. No wonder, within a short time span, in anthropological terms, we have become the most dominant species on the planet, and perhaps in our solar system. We are born with a multitude of highly complex and well-developed skills that make us human, one of the biggest wonders of the natural world. But, somewhere along our lives, we start getting mixed messages from our surroundings which make us doubt our innate abilities and instincts – think fear, shame, guilt, jealousy, social norms, roles, and the glitter of money. The purpose of this book is to make you aware of such noises around you which might have dimmed your natural song, and to help you reconnect to your unhindered selves so that you can shine the way you were meant to. This book is designed to completely unravel any threads (chapter/concept) you might pull (read/ practice). All the chapters in the book are highly interlinked, and yet each chapter talks about a different facet of life and gives you deep insights into specific attributes of your mentality. After reading each chapter, you will find specific exercises that will help you work on some important area of your life, and you will see that your work on one area will easily complement that on another because just like these exercises life is also a blend of all these facets. This is much like different religions which might have different sets of preaching, but all of which ultimately lead you to the same place.

I've been a curious observer of the human mind since childhood, and I still remember sitting by myself and observing the odd behavior of adults in bewilderment. At that time, I was still untouched by the corruption that we face in our lives. I could simply see through the farce and the lies that everyone was telling themselves. I wondered when I could see through them so clearly, why they couldn't see through their own actions? Why were they giving into the pressure of society, blaming others in the family for their undesirable situations, and intoxicating their bodies with substances that were so repulsive to me?

As I was growing up, I too started falling victim to the deafening noises that surrounded me. These noises kept increasing as I got older. It was much lesser when I was a child, but it had completely engulfed me by the time I reached adulthood. Have you ever experienced being in a room where the music volume is slowly turned up in increments, but you don't notice what's happening? By the time the music is too loud, you've stopped noticing it, and you realize how loud the music really was only when it suddenly stops. Try this at home if you haven't experienced this for yourself. Doesn't this sound similar to the tale of the frog in the boiling water? The story goes that if you put a frog in boiling water, it jumps out suddenly. Whereas if you put the frog in cold water and slowly turn up the heat, the frog doesn't realize that it is being boiled alive, and eventually dies. From this we can understand that we get used to the noise and adjust to the new normal until we drink the Kool-Aid.

While growing up I had no idea about how to work on myself. All I was doing with my life was what my parents, teachers, and friends had taught me. I was supposed to behave in specific ways in front on my parents, teachers, and other elders. A lot of things of were pre-decided for me. I was unaware of the reasons for certain choices that I was making–clothes to wear, people to befriend, things to do to look cool in my friend circle, etc. This made me feel hurt, angry, and resentful though I had no idea why I was feeling like that. This was followed by blame and criticism; all that was going wrong in my life was someone else's fault. Without the tools that could help me look clearly inside me, I was lost in the woods of my mind. It's only through meditation that I realized how I could cancel this noise and become connected to the real fabric of my existence and my conscious reality. This book is extremely close to my heart, and it is my attempt to share with the world the experiences and insights that I've gained through my journey in meditation and self-reflection and through my training in psychology and life coaching.

This book is about the thirteen keys that can help you unlock the doors to your inner being – "The unfettered being that you are, capable of greatness, free from the baggage of blame, grudge, and envy." You will see that in most of these chapters, I lay a lot of emphasis on the influence of family and culture in shaping our lives, and most of the times I do so negatively. This is not coming from a place of blame or spite. I simply want to highlight that we have a choice about whether or not to accept life for what it is. The exercises at the end of each chapter are designed to help you dissolve and transform the "drama, blame, judgement, negative self-talk, self-doubt, insecurity, anger, and shame" that you might be carrying inside you as a result of your past experiences. How much you take from this book is up to you. Remember, I'm only showing you the way, but the actual work has to be done by you. In order to draw the maximum benefit from this book, you have to be honest with yourself at every step. Be vulnerable, take the necessary actions, have those honest conversations and discussions that you have been putting off for years. *Only if you're ready to make the effort should you read on. Otherwise, this book will be nothing more than a good read on a lazy Sunday afternoon. If this is your intent, I highly recommend returning this book back to the store from where you bought it.* On the other hand, if you are committed and determined to find something new about yourself then this book will take you on a rollercoaster of emotions. It will unlock the pathways in your mind that have been buried deep under all the noise. I'd like to point out that in this book I have discussed my own experiences and those of my clients to help explain various situations and concepts. Though the experiences described in the book are borrowed from real life, I have changed the names of the people involved to protect their identity.

The purpose of this book is to help you reclaim the

power that lies inside you. Many times in our lives we find ourselves in situations where we feel helpless with people around us. We erroneously conclude that our lives will work once they change. We end up focusing our precious time and energy on affecting change in our partners, children, or parents. By doing so, we essentially give up our own power. This book shows you that you don't need others to change in order for the situation to transform in a mutually beneficial way. The change begins with you yourself. I guarantee that this book is the answer to your problems. I say this because I grew up in a family of five. We knew each other inside out, so we all were playing the game of eliciting certain responses from each other to satisfy the needs inside us. We were living in a stagnant cesspool of drama, blame, judgement, anger, insecurity, and shame. But the moment I took charge of my own thoughts and behaviors, and refused to participate in the wrestle, it completely shook the fine balance that had been developed over the years. Since change brings uncertainty, it is an uncomfortable experience. The family system is like a black hole wanting to suck you in, forcing you to adhere to the old ways of being. However, when I stood my ground firmly, I saw everyone change along with me. The never-ending karmic cycle of the family was broken forever. I didn't have to force others to change; all that I did was take charge of my own actions and emotions.

Given below is a famous painting depicting a tale of truth vs. lies. I think this aptly describes how our true self is lost inside our own minds and how lies roam around masquerading as the truth.

The Naked Truth - "Truth coming out of her well", by Jean-Léon Gérôme, 1896.

The painting tells the story of a chance meeting between Truth and Lie one summery day.

Lie said to Truth, "It's such a marvelous day!"

Truth looked up at the sky and sighed in contentment for the day was really beautiful.

They spent a lot of time together, ultimately arriving beside a well.

Lie said to Truth, "The water is very nice here, let's take a bath together."

Truth, once again suspicious, tested the water and discovered that it indeed was very nice.

They undressed and started bathing. Suddenly, Lie came out of the water, put on Truth's clothes, and ran away. A furious Truth came out of the well and ran everywhere to find Lie and get her clothes back.

The world, seeing Truth naked, turned its gaze away in contempt and rage. Poor Truth returned to the well and disappeared forever, hiding there in shame.

Since then Lie travels around the world dressed as Truth, satisfying the needs of society, because the world, in any case, harbors no wish at all to meet a naked Truth.

THE ABYSS

It was a cloudy, gloomy, and sultry July morning in New Delhi. The monsoon was in full swing. It had been raining incessantly for five days. The rain was beginning to abate, but the air felt heavy. The exhausting heat wave and the humidity made the weather unbearable. The ancient water drainage system of the city fails to match up to the test of the monsoon every year, and floods the city with dirty sewage water. My life wasn't much different; I had too many emotions running through my mind which over flooded every inch of my consciousness. The burden of negative thoughts was too heavy, making me feel pressured every second of the day.

Human life is a gift read a plaque hung outside my co-worker's cubicle at the dingy office of the IT company I worked in. It had been hanging precariously in front of my eyes, and across the aisle, since last year. Far from being an inspiration, the sign seemed to mock my everyday existence. No one except me knew how nothing ever worked in my life, whereas everyone else around me seemed to do just fine. I was stuck in the same job for the last three years without any increase in pay or position.

My employer doesn't acknowledge the talent that I bring on the table; being completely inept in office politics, I will never be noticed by my bosses; it's way too competitive out there, I will never succeed; these were the thoughts that rang through my head every time I saw that ominous quote hanging across my cubicle.

At twenty-five, I should have been on my way to becoming a Director by now. How else would I become the President of a company by the time I was forty? On the other hand, my siblings were doing exceedingly well in their careers. My brother had landed a handsome job at a large multinational corporation, and my sister had been handpicked to head a high-impact team at her workplace. I was a failure; immersed in negativity, stuck in the defeating vortex of comparison, self-doubt, stress, anxiety, and shame.

The traffic in Delhi can be sinister. It has been known to swallow many a lives, and mine wasn't any exception. I was stuck in the traffic for two hours on my way to work today. I reached office just as the daily brief with Steve, our department head, got over. My boss, Sam, came to my desk and gave me an earful about how my lack of punctuality was setting a bad example for other employees, and how my absence in the meeting today didn't go down very well with Steve. Over the last one month I had been consistently late for work. I just hadn't been able to drag myself out of bed in time. The timing of this really sucked because we had our annual appraisal the next day. This entire year, I had put in a lot of work, and I had been instrumental in winning the largest account for the company. I was hoping that my recent tardiness wouldn't cost me the promotion that I had been coveting for the last so many years.

On my way to work the next day, I was again caught up in the traffic. I had started from home an hour early. I didn't want to get late again, especially not on "Appraisal Day". I was stuck in the same spot for twenty minutes with the cars barely moving, when I noticed a flyer on my passenger seat. It read – Take control of your life, a 3-day meditation workshop to revamp your life. It had been handed to me by a monk in saffron robes, who had accosted me while I had been walking towards my car from my apartment. He had insisted that I keep this flyer, and I had flung it inside my car. Those of you who haven't been to Delhi should know that people here have a habitual need to honk in the traffic, even when the vehicle ahead of them has no space to move. My trance was broken by the horn blaring loudly from the car behind me. I realized that I had been staring at the flyer for the last ten minutes, day dreaming about how I want my life to look like if I had a chance to consciously recreate it.

I reached office early and parked my car with a sigh of relief. When you're not pressed for time, you start observing your surroundings more closely. Entering the big glass lobby of our office building, I noticed the beautiful light fixtures that hung from the ceiling for the first time. I bumped into one of my colleagues, Rick, who was standing in the lobby. After exchanging pleasantries, he gave me a piece of news that really raised my hopes. Apparently, the rumor doing the rounds was that Sam, the Head of Department for Business Development, who was also my boss, had resigned. According to the rumor mills, she had been offered a job by a competing organization. That meant with the amount of work I had put into my job this year, they would have to consider giving me the reins of the department at last. I was the natural successor to Sam. These thoughts raced through my mind as I started walking towards my cubicle.

Appraisal time was here. I arrived at the conference room ten minutes earlier and picked up a comfortable spot to sit in. We entertain a lot of clients in our office, however, I noticed that the AV system in our conference room was outdated. That is the first thing I would fix when I am offered Sam's position, I thought. I noticed Sam standing outside the conference room, engaged in an animated discussion with Rick, and there they stayed for the next five minutes. Apparently, Sam had not realized that I was already in the meeting room, so I stepped outside to make my presence known. On noticing me, both Sam and Rick entered the room and got seated in front of me. Without beating around the bush, Sam began with the agenda of the meeting. I was taken aback as I had not expected Rick to participate in my appraisal. These discussions were supposed to be confidential between the employee and the manager. I was very uncomfortable with the whole setting, and was about to express my discomfort, when Sam broke the news that she was leaving the company, and that Rick had been asked to take her position. Her words fell on me like a ton of bricks. That was so unfair! The way it was being handled was downright unprofessional. I zoned out of the conversation, and the rest of Sam's words fell on deaf ears, sliding off me. My eyes stayed fixed on the white board behind Sam and Rick. I kept going back to the countless nights I had spent at office all by myself, and how I had been solely instrumental in bringing in several high-profile clients to our organization. I knew Sam and Steve had never really taken a liking to me. All these thoughts about office politics, competition, and brown nosing the bosses kept on flooding my mind. My mind kept wandering back to that advertisement I had seen when I was stuck in traffic today. How I wish I too could take control of my life.

And then, without me consciously realizing what I was saying, two words slipped out of my mouth – "I quit."

THE LIGHT

It was a hot Monday morning, the sun had already risen half way to the zenith. A week had passed since I had quit my job, and I had been sleeping in late again. There is a strange guilt that comes in with waking up late. The hustle and bustle of the morning is already dead by the time you are up. The silence of the afternoon reminds you that the world is up and about their work, contributing to society, working their way through their lives. It brings on a cold sensation that you're missing out on something, missing out on life.

My thoughts kept on returning to the past three years of my life. Had I not quit, I would have been already at work for hours by now, running from one end of the office to the other, trying to manage my ten-member operations team. With tight deadlines to meet, I would have been in a constant tug of war with my employees, blaming myself, caught in the spiral of sink or sail all day long. Blame, both internal and external, were my constant companions. I had completely sacrificed my life for the job, working from 7 a.m. to 8 p.m., even on many Saturdays. I had no time to meet people; no love life. I had been chugging five cups of coffee every day; had gained fifteen pounds in the last one year alone. What had I become?

My gaze fell on a bright yellow paper kept over a stack of files on my study table. It was the flyer about the mediation course that had been handed to me by the white-bearded monk a week ago. I was desperate to try anything to get my life back on track. Maybe I could become enlightened and gain some deep insights into the inner workings of the human mind through this meditation course, as was professed by popular media. Or maybe I would meet some nice people, perhaps some good-looking guy, make some new contacts. I had nothing to lose. So I decided to give the course a try. I was immediately filled with optimism, the one that comes when you're about to embark on a new journey with over-simplified assumptions. I contacted the phone number listed on the flyer, and learnt that the next workshop was starting in a couple of days, so I registered immediately. And then, I realized in horror that I didn't have anything appropriate in my wardrobe to wear for something like this. For the last three years, my life had been consumed by work 24/7, and the only things that fit me anymore were my office clothes. I was too lazy to go out shopping, and ended up borrowing a couple of comfortable outfits from my sister.

I entered the hall where the course was going to be held. The huge hall was filled with yoga mats lined up neatly in several rows. I reached the venue a bit early and found the hall practically empty. People kept trickling in slowly as I settled down on the yoga mat placed in the center of the first row. In about half an hour the room was full of old people and housewives. Oh my God! Where had I come? Is this place even for me? What was I trying to do? Then a good-looking man in his thirties came onstage and introduced himself and the course in a deep, calming voice. For the next three days, we were promised a journey from our everyday mundane anxieties to a place of peace and wisdom. We were told to close our eyes, focus on our breathing, and to thank our ancestors. After ten minutes of meditation, my thoughts were everywhere but on my breathing. I was feeling the vacuum due to the absence of external stimuli. I was having the urge to check my phone for emails. I had to remind myself that I was no longer employed and had no work-related emails to answer. My mind was constantly taking me back to work: *I'm sure they will feel my absence at work; I wonder how Rick is handling the new position.*

I had great difficulty disengaging my mind, and could focus on my breathing only sporadically. The aroma of freshly baked muffins was coming from the table near me, and the anticipation of having a muffin after the class was overwhelming me. I was constantly yawning, itching, and fidgeting. The last thing I remember was that we were told to lie down on our mats for the rest of the session for meditation. I felt a tug on my right shoulder as I awakened from deep sleep. I had slept through the last session! The person sitting next to me was trying to wake me up for the conclusion of the class. When I sat up, I saw the entire class was waiting for me to wake up. I was filled with a deep sense of shame and embarrassment. I felt like I had made a fool of myself in front of the whole class, and I didn't want to come back for the class tomorrow! The instructor congratulated us for finishing the most important day of the course, and he announced that even if we didn't feel like we had any profound experience that day, but it was all part of the plan, and that we should come again the next day for a real breakthrough. Since I had already paid up for the course and had nothing better to do with my time, I reluctantly agreed to come the next day.

I sat on the same mat the next day. In multiday sessions or conferences, I have seen the same phenomenon repeating itself every single time. People like to return to the same seating arrangement they had randomly chosen the previous day. I guess there's something in the human mind that craves the familiar for it makes us feel secure. The day started with the *Chakra Meditation*. Apparently there are seven chakras in the human body. We were instructed to sit crossed-legged and feel our chakras, starting from the root to the crown, and experience a ball of energy behind the navel. The whole purpose of this exercise was to balance and align our chakras. I felt a sudden impulse of restlessness, wanting to get up. Was this even scientifically proven? It was all in the realm of touchy-feely non-science, with no logical backing. What was I doing wasting my time with these self-proclaimed gurus? Meanwhile, the class progressed to the *Breathing Meditation*, where we had to focus on our breathing and let go of thoughts. Within a couple of minutes my mind started to wander: My friend of fifteen years was expecting a baby, and I was supposed to organize a baby shower for her; I was given a gold star in the fifth grade for scoring the highest points in a spelling bee; there was a cute boy in school whom I always wanted to date; I was so clueless when I had just started my first job. The chain of thoughts was broken when I felt a numbness and discomfort in my leg, which was lying stationary for a while. I opened my eyes to see varied expressions on people's faces. Some had a serene look on their faces, some looked serious with creased foreheads, and some were smiling. The last exercise of the day again was the *Yoga Nidra* – sleeping meditation. The instructor guided us to relax each part of our body one by one, starting from the head to the toes. By the time he asked us to focus on the arms I was already asleep. A sudden loud noise thankfully woke me up before the exercise was over. From the horrid smell, I realized that the person next to me had just farted. I avoided breathing deeply and started to take in short, shallow breaths. This was so disgusting. Why don't people know how to conduct themselves in public? But on the whole, my experience on the second day wasn't as bad as the day before.

On the final day of the course, we began with the *Metta Meditation* – also called the loving kindness meditation. The instructor told us to feel love and kindness for ourselves and for others in our lives. We had to visualize acts of kindness towards all the people we interacted with on a daily basis. In this day and age, where we're constantly competing with ourselves and with the people around us, the feeling of compassion is not practiced often. I felt a deep sense of love for the people in the room, even for the person who had farted in the room the day before. After sometime we got into practicing *Taichi,* which involves very slow and elongated movements. Apparently, this directs a smooth flow of our Qi -the Life Energy—through our bodies. To my amazement, the slow movements of the body helped me relax my thoughts. I enjoyed the present and wasn't thinking about the past or the future. We also practiced other forms of meditation like the *Mantra Meditation* and the *Walking Meditation.* The day finally ended with the *Yoga Nidra.* For the first time, I was able to go through the entire exercise without falling asleep. At the end of the day, I was relaxed and balanced as if the constant chatter in my mind was somewhat silent, and there seemed to be some space for me to stay in the now. If a little bit of a difference in the mind could make me feel this way, what would a whole lot of difference feel like? My voice was markedly softer when I greeted my classmates on my way out. While driving home, I didn't listen to any music, but I felt rejuvenated, like one usually feels after a long vacation. I reached home and slept peacefully for a couple of hours.

THE AWAKENING

The chirping of birds woke me up. It was 6 a.m. in the morning. I had been sleeping like a baby. I felt peaceful in a way I hadn't felt for many years. I wanted to stay inside the warm embrace of my blanket, feeling safe and secure in my little cocoon. My lethargy was suddenly interrupted when I realized that I had an intruder in the room. A magpie was sitting on my nightstand, and it felt like it was wishing me a good morning in whatever language Magpie's speak. I realized that I had left a window open in my room the previous night. I kept lying in bed to observe my guest. Oblivious to the fact that I was watching it, the bird perched itself on the bowl of snacks that I had kept on my nightstand and pecked at its breakfast. When I got up though the bird became aware of my presence and flew away. It was an unusual experience. Not every day do I wake up to the sight of a bird next to my bed.

I made myself a steaming cup of coffee and went out to the patio. It had been raining the previous night. All the plants looked lush green covered with water droplets that gleamed in the sunlight. The stillness of the morning, the beam of light falling on the plants that was highlighting different shades of green, and the crispness of the morning, all of it made me feel at one with my surroundings. I observed how still my mind was, took a deep breath, and sat down in my chair. Peace stole over me, and instead of riding my emotions, for once I was looking at them from a distance. The chatter of meaningless emotions was gone for the moment; it was as if I was wearing one of those noise-cancellation headphones. I knew I had to find a job soon, and I knew that the process might take several weeks. But instead of feeling anxious, I could plan ahead calmly. I knew I needed to apply for jobs online, reach out to my friends, appear for interviews, etc. But to my surprise the process wasn't bothering me. Instead, I felt this pull to practice meditation to realign my life. I felt like an observer of my own feelings; it was as if I was observing myself from a higher perch, as if my observing mind and deciding mind were two distinct entities. It seemed that all my fears and emotions were arising from my deciding mind, while my observing mind could view these dispassionately and choose how to react. Over the next couple of months, I went neck deep into a world of self-exploration. And, this turned out to be the best decision that I had ever taken for it transformed my life.

The biggest takeaway from my self-exploration journey is the fact that we're conscious creators of our human experiences. Whether we're aware of it or not, our sensory and extrasensory perceptions are bombarded by stimuli at all times. Our version of reality is really stitched from the fabric of our own interpretations of these stimuli.

This means that most of what we term as good or bad, positive or negative, happy or sad, right or wrong, possible or impossible, is a matter of choice. "It's all in the mind." Each of us has the ability to filter what we want to let into our minds, and thus consciously create our realities. We just haven't learned to get tuned to that frequency. For the most part, we go about our lives without realizing that we have a choice.

The human brain is the most complex biochemical machine ever created on planet earth. Think of the first time you learnt to use a complex machine. Let's say when you first learnt to drive a car or use a computer, it took you a lot of practice to get full control of the machine. Without tools to steer your brain in the right direction, you're just a passive rider; and never in control. The following chapters in this book are my insights from years of meditative practice and working on myself. I have found certain tools that can help your inner mind regain the reins of your conscious reality.

The thirteen phenomena explained in the following chapters are the common threads of thoughts that make us fall into the spiral of negative beliefs and create an underwhelming reality. Merely reading about these concepts might not help someone realize the power of these techniques. The exercises described in each chapter will help you really apply these concepts in your everyday life, and help you gain a deep insight into their limiting nature. It takes discipline and practice to tame your mind and turn it into a friend. If you follow the exercises mentioned in the chapters, I promise it will transform your life in ways you never thought possible. You have been living the same life for all these years. All I ask is that you give twenty-six days to try out a new life with these thirteen principles.

Best of luck as you embark on this beautiful journey!

CHAPTER 1

Stop the Bloody DRAMA!

"**O**bserve more, listen more, and speak less. Not everything needs a reaction. Step away from drama!"

Drama is overhyping of a state. It is a tendency to exaggerate or to lie about the gravity of a situation, or rather that "sky is falling" mentality. We all have met people who make mountains out of mole hills. We all crave for attention consciously or subconsciously. Have you ever wondered why a new job that begins with high hopes and with the zeal to perform often ends in quitting or getting fired? Drama is most often seen in relationships. It all starts on a good note, but then it ends with bitterness, betrayal, and separation. A marriage which begins with love ends in hatred. A business partnership that begins with trust, ends with betrayal. Family relations end with discord and ill feelings. If there was an independent observer watching our lives play out as a stage show, he would have been able to point out the dramas each of us played to bring about the calamitous ends. We take the drama in our everyday life so lightly that we fail to see its repercussions. None of us want to admit that we all create drama to different degrees in our lives.

Let me share the story of one of my clients. Mike is in his thirties, working at a large organization as a mid-manager. He came to me to get coached about his professional growth. Nobody seemed to understand and appreciate his caliber, he said. He should have been a high-flying executive. However he was stuck in a dead-end job. He was a victim of his circumstances, and wasn't able to succeed in life due to external factors. He was waiting for his professional career to take off, and for everything to be okay. He was frustrated with life and with himself. While we began with the intention to cover the areas in which Mike's skills could be enhanced, it became apparent that what really needed most work was his attitude. In my sessions with Mike, we discovered that he had been a very successful student in school and college. To him, it was a given that he would be at the top in all his endeavors. He was shocked and disappointed when some of his classmates, who had been less successful than him as a student, had become more successful than him in life, whereas success seemed to evade him. As a result, he avoided meeting his former classmates. What would they think of him and his lack of success? He was afraid to face them. He only made friends with people who validated his superiority. He couldn't seem to get along with people who were more successful than him. He constantly ruminated on his past glory and made his achievements known to everyone he met. He was easily bored in his job, which he anyways thought was not up to his standard. He talked, walked, and behaved like a boss. He snubbed people during discussions, and at work, as all of them were fools in his eyes, and he always had the most valid points to make. He came home frustrated, and expected that this wife would submit to him. He had no time for her emotions and for the petty things she had going on in her life. They had an unsatisfactory married life, and were on the verge of separation. After numerous coaching sessions, Mike realized to his dismay that he was running a "drama". He was stuck in a make-believe world where he was the best in everything he did. And as a result, he was paying a heavy price. During our sessions he finally accepted that he was in a denial mode, and that he was the one creating the "drama" in his life. *How many of us can somewhat relate to Mike?*

At the heart of all drama there is a need for payoff. All forms of drama usually originate from one of the following reasons:

<u>Low self-esteem/worth</u> may lead us to either behave like victims or to overstate our achievements to create an illusion of worth in the eyes of others. Cynthia had a minor cleft lip since birth which made her very conscious of her appearance. She was low on self-esteem because of her perceived lack of beauty. She even attributed her lack of friends in school to her looks. In order to prove her own worth, she became an ace student, and went on to be a successful entrepreneur. Her identify is now driven by her success in life. When she meets other good-looking people, she is obnoxiously boastful of her success. Her "drama" of success is simply a veil to cover her lack of self-worth for being "ugly".

<u>When we avoid venturing out of our comfort zone,</u> it may lead us to create drama with others. Blaming other people or circumstances gives us a way to hide our own shortcomings. Tony has been dating Monica for the last five years, but is afraid of commitment. Instead of working on his fears, he is creating a drama in front of his parents, friends, and Monica that he needs to be more stable in his job before getting married.

<u>A need for adrenaline rush</u> can make us intensify relationships too soon. Dramatic breakups, passionate

makeups, yelling, throwing things around, these are common dramatic phenomena in relationships. People in such relationships judge their love on the intensity of the rush they feel by creating this drama. These relationships lack an empathetic ear and a compassionate heart. These are essentially self-serving relationships which are kept alive by the mutual need for excitement. Instead of basing their relationship on understanding, these people get their rush by proving their superiority over their partners and by subduing each other.

<u>To draw the attention of others</u> we exaggerate and spin stories. These are the people who are hard to miss in a social setting. Such individuals are lively and dramatic, and they draw attention to themselves with their enthusiasm, clothes, their appearance and openness. On the surface, they are the life of the party, and they seem interested in others, but deep down, they have an insatiable need for attention and approval. They will be persistent in their efforts to draw attention, and will feel helpless and anxious if their need is not met. The biggest price such people pay is that they are unable to form healthy interpersonal relationships.

We often get blinded about how we live our lives, and don't even realize how we get caught up in our own drama. There are many ways in which we're creating drama, overstating your misery to portray yourself as a victim; stating again and again how life has been so difficult, how your pain is greater than that of others; calling ten people when you break up with someone, etc. Other forms of drama include overstating your accomplishments, overhyping your own or someone's good or misfortune, or overstating an emergency to prove how your leadership abilities saved the day. Teenagers create drama by proving how cool they are. Drama can even take extreme forms of self or substance abuse, over-eating, or any other obsessive-compulsive disorders.

When we're not creating drama, we're busy falling into the trap of drama that others create. The group-think in drama is especially hard to evaluate objectively and mitigate. Take for instance a situation where the son of the family is dating someone who has different values from them. Generally, the family will create drama by evaluating and dissecting every action of the girl. They will discuss the issue amongst themselves and validate each other. This drama results in negative energy in the group, and the family may never be able to accept and bond with the girl. The snowballing effect will cause the son to eventually question his girlfriend's behavior. He may try to control and change her to please his family. The family's drama has now fully come in the way of their relationship, and they will now question each other's intentions. The next stage will be fights on an everyday basis, emotional distancing between the couple, and eventual separation.

I want to give a special mention to a particularly dangerous kind of drama, gossiping. Have you ever felt a cold vibe from an acquaintance at a party or at your workplace? It seems there is something negative that everyone else knows about you, and that makes you feel isolated. In such cases, you may later find out that you've been a victim of someone's gossip. Most likely it all started with a drama queen/king, who had nothing better to do, and was having a cheap thrill by exaggerating or by lying about your affairs. Gossip is just another form of bullying, and with the advent of social media, its effects are especially far-reaching and devastating. Samantha was fifteen when her family relocated to a new city. She went out on a date with a boy whom she liked. The next day the boy, wanting to act cool, bragged about "last night" with his buddies. He got caught up in his drama, and spun lies about the girl's promiscuity. The word got out fast, and she was ostracized in her school. This mental harassment eventually led the girl to commit suicide. When the truth finally came out, the boy was suspended from school, and he served time in a juvenile home.

Remember, you reap what you sow. More often than not, if you get involved in gossiping, it will come back and bite you in your behind when the curtain is raised and reality comes to light. Gossiping also isolates the gossiper; people eventually learn to see through the gossip mongers, and may resent them.

Drama keeps a relationship intense, whether with yourself or with others. People who like this intensity are addicted to drama. The problem with any kind of drama is that it removes us from reality, it clouds our perception about the situation. Drama such as gossiping, or blaming, is a façade we create. This keeps us from knowing our true selves, our fears, emotions, and shortcomings. When we create drama, we relinquish the control to objectively view our situation and realize what we could do differently; we get engaged in habits that provide petty mental relief instead of focusing on real solutions or meaningful growth. This closes all pathways of learning from our mistakes, and prevents us from growing as human beings. If we don't learn from our mistakes, we will keep recreating the same situation over and over again, eliciting the same response from ourselves and others. We will be stuck in a vicious cycle, and never realize how we can behave differently or chose differently in a future situation. This will result in us getting overwhelmed in our lives, and not knowing the way out of any mess. The person who creates drama will never be able to forge true and meaningful relationships with themselves or others.

Here are some traits of people who create drama:

1. **Overemotional reaction** – Such people amplify their reactions to an event to gain the attention of others. Say for instance little Johnny is unwell. As soon as his dramatic parents come to know about it, they will create a scene in the house, and will pass this news to their friends and relatives, creating hysteria. Instead of taking care of Johnny, the parents are using this situation as an opportunity to meet their own need of drama.

2. **Attention-seeking behavior** – Dramatic people usually have a dire need for attention, and can spin stories to meet their needs. These people overhype their

miseries and successes with the intent of becoming the center of attention. For example, Joan gives a lot to charity, but makes sure that everyone knows about it in full details. Another example is Mary who went on a vacation to Europe last summer, and showed off her pictures to anyone she met. She even manages to steer all her conversations to that trip so that she can boast about her luxury vacation and become the center of attention.

3. **Manipulation** – People prone to drama manipulate others with shame, guilt, or fear. Most parents know how to tame young children with the fear of punishment. When the children become adults and start their own families, the same parents subconsciously keep their children tied to their apron strings with guilt and shame by saying how the children don't tend to their needs, or don't visit enough. Another form of manipulation is to be overly good to someone with an ulterior motive. These people may indulge others with expensive gifts, compliments, and general niceness, all with the intention to make others lower their guards and make them more prone to their manipulation. Many movies have been made on this premise.

4. **Jealously and insecurity** – People who create drama are overly competitive. They are jealous and insecure of other people who don't surrender to their leadership. They will wage a one-sided, toxic, personal battle against their adversaries, without letting them even know about it. They will take it upon themselves

to bad-mouth others to lower their social standing in society. The feeling of power they drive from doing so helps them maintain their hierarchy in the social order. We see this in families, small groups, offices, and even in the highest echelons of power.

5. **Murky intent** – Dramatic people like to remain in the good books of others as this gives them more avenues to further their agenda. Such people will be overly inquisitive about other's lives as they are always on the hunt for juicy gossip which they can pass along to others. They like to play mind games, pitting one against another, with the intent of coming out as the pack leader. It would not be a stretch to call this borderline socio-path behavior.

When I first read about Dr. Stephen Karpman's drama triangle, it helped me see clearly how we all indulge in such behavior.

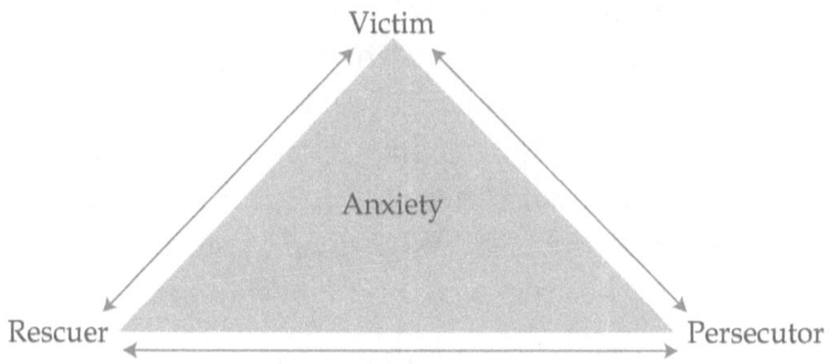

The Victim is someone who plays the victim card, and sees themselves as oppressed, weak, powerless, and helpless. They want super-sensitive treatment from others.

They deny responsibility for all that is going on in their lives and throw blame outwards. They have issues in making decision themselves, solving problems, and in creating a satisfying life on their own. They fail to realize their self-perpetuating behavior. They always need a rescuer to come and save them from a sticky situation, like Rapunzel who was waiting to be saved by her knight in shining armor.

The Rescuer is someone who feels good about themselves by helping or taking care of others. They live in a co-dependent relationship with victims who allow themselves to be rescued. For a rescuer, it's very difficult to ask for help as they take pride in playing the hero. Rescuers are often overworked, tired, and feel like martyrs. But underneath all that, resentment grows inside them. For example, grown-up children (rescuers) take pride in caring for their aging parents (victims), who act as if they need help at every turn.

The Persecutors are trapped in the stance of "it's all your fault". They are critical of the victim, and can be highly controlling. They yell and criticize, but don't actually solve any problems. Take for instance, dominating parents who tend to find faults with their children all the time – "Why did you fall from the bike? Why didn't you ride properly?" Or "Look, what has happened now, it's all your fault."

All of us create drama, to varying extents, and swing to and fro from one role to another in order to meet some personal (often unconscious) needs without ever coming out of the triangle. Each of us has a preferred role which we fall into every now and then though we exhibit the traits of all the above roles. Victims need a savior, rescuers depend on victims to let them be saviors, and persecutors want to find scapegoats. This is an exhausting way of living life.

In dysfunctional families, the culture is to form triangular relationships with their gossip and drama. Family members bond with each other by talking about other family members behind their backs. They bond with each other by finding a common person to criticize, almost as if they are taking revenge on the targeted person. This is a vicious cycle that creates dysfunctionality, and results in family members having confused relationships with each other.

(Father ⇆ Mother) The couple's relationship is based on drama as they are constantly blaming and resenting each other. Their relationship lacks compassion and understanding. They execute drama by fighting over petty issues like who takes out the trash, whose fault it is, whose emotions are valid, etc.

(Mother ⇆ Child) The mother now tries to isolate the father by bringing the child to her side. She tells the child how insensitive or incapable the father is, thus poisoning the mind of their child. It gives the woman a sense of power over her husband.

(Child ⇆ Father) The child has been manipulated into feeling responsible for comforting her mother, to resonate with her mother's emotions about the father. The child will try to rescue the mother from the father every time there is a disagreement. In this family, everyone is manipulating each other for their personal need to gain attention and security at the expense of the other.

Using the example of the same family, let's try to understand how the relationships would have played out if the family wasn't ridden by drama.

(Mother ⇆ Father) When the mother and father had a disagreement it was handled in private between the two. The parents were compassionate and understood each other. They stood up to their promises, and presented a united front to their child. Important matters between the couple, like finances, relationship, etc. were not disclosed to the child since the child is powerless in these matters.

(Parents ⇆ Child) The parents were mindful of the impact these discussions would have on the child's psychology. The child was not burdened with adult problems, and was fully supported and cared for. The child was allowed to focus her energy on playing, studying, and growing up so that she can become a mature, sensitive, and mindful adult. In this case, no triangular relationships were formed and no one was talking behind each other. No one was forming unnecessary and unhealthy attachments. A very important hierarchy was followed, which is, I (personal needs, not wishes and desires) → Partner and couple relationship needs (mother and father stand for each other front of their children) → Needs of the children → Friends, family, relatives, and society.

Drama generally tends to put us in a survival mode.

If you were brought up in a chaotic, dramatic household, it's easy to get absorbed in the drama, and it is difficult to detach yourself from it. Or, you may have found a way to stay grounded, and are very aware of how the drama plays out. The only way out of drama is to recognize what role you and others play, when and how. If you keep giving into your impulses, you create a havoc in the family environment. The malaise of drama is to keep you engaged in the chaos so that you don't get the chance to address the real issue. Say for instance, Eric is fifteen years old, and is going camping with his class. Before Eric begins planning his trip, his parents who have been dictating Eric's life, take charge. They have already started packing his clothes, snacks, medicines, and gear. They are making frantic phone calls to friends and family to gather information about how far the campgrounds are from the highway, where the nearest restaurants are, or what hospitals are closest. Eric is supposed to call them every two hours and inform them about his well-being and whereabouts. When Eric misses a couple of phone calls, the parents panic and start calling up his friends and teachers. Here Eric is sucked into his parent's drama, and lets them take the lead. He even complies with the impositions of his parents and diligently responds to their phone calls every couple of hours. Eric is falsely believing that this overprotective nature of his parents stems from pure parental love. He doesn't see through their drama of "trying to feel important" by staying relevant in Eric's life. They make a victim out of Eric, and make him believe that he needs them to come to his rescue. If Eric has a small, harmless accident, the parents will switch continuously back and forth between the roles of prosecutor and rescuer - "I told you to be careful and not do this. Look now what has happened," or "Don't worry, we're here now, you'll be fine."

I want to now illustrate how Eric's family would have behaved if they had not fallen in the pit of drama. Eric told his parents about his trip, and the parents volunteered their help. Eric packed his bag and planned his trip. He asked his parents for suggestions, and the parents helped as asked. The parents didn't turn Eric's trip into their own agenda, and stayed focused on their own affairs. They mirrored the level of excitement that Eric was feeling for his trip. Eric, in turn, gave them the phone numbers of a couple of his friends for emergency situations. The parents were mindful to not disturb Eric when he was camping with his friends. When Eric came back from his trip and told his parents about his little accident, the parents showed their concern. They didn't ask for unnecessary details as Eric was obviously fine. Neither the parents nor Eric was stuck in drama in this case. They showed their love and care by respecting each other's emotions and boundaries, and yet stood by each other.

Now it's time to see how you play the drama in your real life, and how you get sucked into other people's drama. The chart below shows the common ways of thinking and acting when you're stuck in a particular role in the drama triangle.

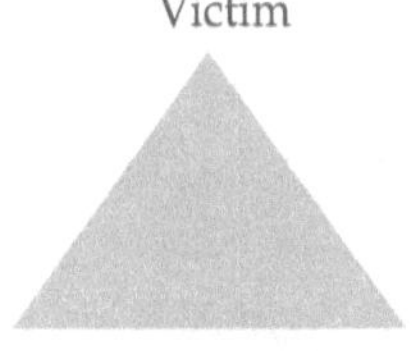
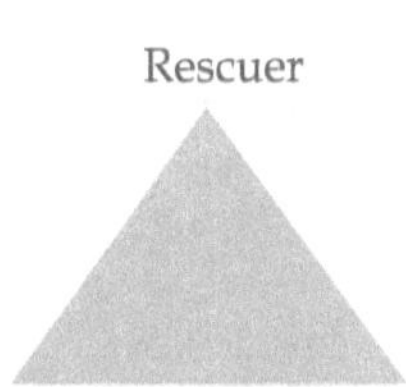
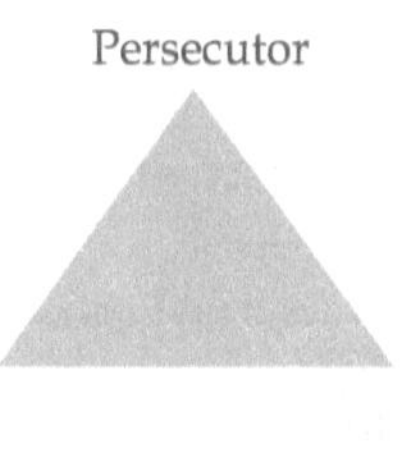

Underlying Beliefs		
I can't	I can handle it	I told you so
I'm so dumb	Poor you	Why don't you listen to me
I'm helpless	I understand	You are always making mistakes
I'm confused	I'll make it better for you	You are not doing this right
It hurts	I'll keep you away from harm	If only you would listen
Help me	I'll always be there for you	I can't forgive you
I can't do this on my own	I'll help you get your act together	You should
What's happening is not fair	Let me do it for you	Why are you always like this
I don't have a choice	I can quickly fix this for you	Stop feeling!
Everyone uses me	I know how to do it, let me	Look at me, I have done it all
I need change	You don't need to be sad, I'm here	You will never protection
Everyone is mean to me	You can always count on me	You don't know anything

Behaviors and feelings		
Feels oppressed, hopeless, incapable, and misunderstood	Supports other at expense of self	Critical, domineering, and bossy
Seeks the validation of the rescuer	Feels guilty and anxious if doesn't rescue	Puts other people down
Doesn't stand up to the attacker	Feels connected and capable when victim is dependent	Blames and finger points
Refuses to make decisions, solve problems, get professional help, do self-care, or change behavior	Provides unsolicited support	Feels anger or resentment
		Fears being out of control
		Rigid in thinking

The first step to change is to create awareness about the role exchange that we're stuck in in our relationships. Take time to introspect, and answer these questions honestly. If you want, you can write your answers in the provided space after each of these questions.

1. Looking at the chart above, can you see a dominant role that you play in your relationships with the following people? Think about how consistent they have been since your childhood.

Relationship	Role I play	Role they play	Desired state (1: un-balanced -10: balanced)
Mother			
Father			
Siblings			
Spouse			
Children			

2. What is the cost you pay to play this role, and what did you get in return?

Cost____

____

____

Benefit____

____

____

3. Now take responsibility of your actions and step out of the drama. The drama that we play with people around us and that is played by others is co-dependent, as described in the drama triangle above. It is an ecosystem where no one will let you change because they are counting on you to play your part in the drama. When you shift, it will cause a disruption in their drama cycle too. They will try to pull you back so that you can continue playing your previous role by punishing you, by shaming you, by making you feel guilty. It might be helpful to employ certain tools to remind yourself of your choice to break this pattern - notes to

yourself stuck on the refrigerator, office desk, or medicine cabinet. You can also have an accountability partner. This is the most challenging step in the change. But once you cross it, it will be uplifting and empowering. You will break the karmic cycle that you've been stuck in since your childhood. You will now be a more balanced, responsible, peaceful, creative, and empowered person. You will also see a drastic improvement in your health, sleep, and overall well-being.

- Be determined about the fact that you don't need drama in your relationships.

- Notice your thoughts or any other triggers.

- Make a note of your self-worth and self-esteem issues.

- "I'm balance and I'm peace in every thought, word, and action" is the affirmation to carry.

With your new understanding about drama, think of the minute shifts that you will bring in your interactions with these individuals, and see how they may resist the change. Try to be as specific as possible (for example, the small shift I made was that I stopped reciprocating when people around me were creating drama. When I was asked for my opinion on their gossip, I would simply refuse to comment. All this while I was affirming to myself that "I'm balance and peace.").

Alternate Beliefs		
<u>VICTIM</u>	<u>RESCUER</u>	<u>PERSECUTOR</u>
I can	You can handle it	Active listening with empathy
I can help myself	You are capable	It's okay to make mistakes
I can do this on my own	I will offer help only where required	Everyone is the best judge of their own situation
I can ask for help when needed	You are capable of making it better for yourself	Forgive others and yourself
I always have choices	I trust you to take care of yourself	There's no one way of doing things
I can create boundaries	I'm here if you need me	I appreciate you
I can take self-care	I'm willing to listen to your problem without making it mine to solve	Carry gratitude
I'm capable of protecting myself		Everyone's unique
I don't have a choice		
Acknowledge your strengths		

Relationship	Note the precise shifts in actions that you can make in these relationships
Mother	
Father	
Siblings	
Spouse	
Children	

Meditation is a must for everyone. I can't overemphasize how simple and yet powerful a tool it is to center and balance your mind. It's only when you practice meditation that you can begin to realize what you've been missing. For people struggling with drama in their lives, stillness meditation is particularly helpful in instilling balance and peace.

CHAPTER 2

Blame, Blame, Blame! Blame Some More!

"**W**hen you blame and criticize others, you are avoiding some truth about yourself."- Deepak Chopra

Blame is to assign responsibility for your misfortunes outside of yourself. Most people in the world indulge in the blame game at some point or the other. For example, I got late to work, but the person whose car broke down and caused the traffic is to blame; I slipped and fell, the person who left the floor wet is the culprit; I burnt that meal because my kids distracted me; I didn't get the promotion because of office politics; God blessed only a few with money and fortune; I don't have the right body type, my genetics are at fault; I'm not able to get a job, the economy is to blame. Blame your partner, neighbor, doctor, shop assistant, technology. The list is endless! Blame, blame, blame!

Why do we blame? Do we even get to know when we blame others? Can blaming be a choice? Blaming is an irrational behavior. Blaming others lets us off the hook. It's too much work to assume responsibility for things that go wrong as that means accepting some truth about ourselves and making uncomfortable changes in our lives. Moreover, blaming others makes us look good to ourselves.

On the other end of the spectrum is the behavior where we assign all blame on ourselves. This is toxic self-criticism. For example, my parents are angry at me because I'm dumb; My family is ashamed of me because I didn't stand up to their expectations; No one likes to be my friend because I'm not interesting; I'm unworthy of respect;

It's okay for someone to throw tantrums at me; Someone took advantage of me because I was too trusting; He was aggressive with me because I provoked him; My son is a bad spouse because I was a bad role model.

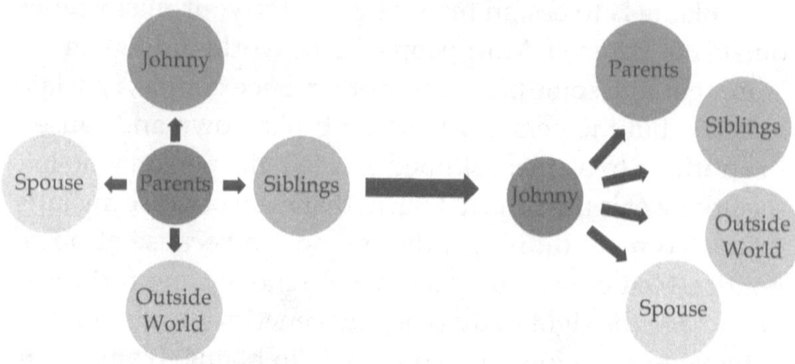

Let me tell you a story here. Johnny's parents were consumed by blame. His mother would constantly criticize and blame the father for not earning enough. The father would blame the mother for constantly criticizing and bickering about every small thing. They both rebuked Johnny with statements like "How dumb of you to do that," or "I'm having a headache because of Johnny." They would belittle Johnny with condescending looks. Due to this environment he could not express his emotions as a child. He felt inconsequential to his parents, and as a result, he developed abandonment issues. Johnny accepted all the blame that his parents' put on him, and believed that he was broken. His parents blamed the world for being crooked as they couldn't succeed in their business. They blamed their own parents for not leaving them with enough inheritance. Johnny's parents never took responsibility for their own lives. They used blame to shield themselves from their own imperfections.

Johnny grew up in an environment where blaming others was the norm. While growing up he learned the most by observing, like any other child would. Like a sponge, he absorbed every minute details about his environment. He learned how he could blame himself and others for everything in life. His behavior reflected that of his parents. He would blame his own parents, wife, siblings, colleagues, and the world at large as he grew up. At the same time, he would blame himself for not being a good son. His habit to blame had become so entrenched in him that it all seemed real to him. Johnny never learnt to accept himself, and instead of facing his intense emotions, learnt to blame others and himself.

Just like Johnny and his family, most of us deny our responsibilities and blame others. Blamers have a few common lines. If she hadn't said that, I wouldn't have done that; He brings out the worst in me; I will change if you do; I yelled at the child in front of everyone because his behavior called for it; It was justified to cuss at the driver on the road because he burst into my lane ahead of me; I have anger management issues because of my dad. Blamers are like children in adult bodies. They will make a hue and cry about the smallest of things they do, and then expect others to keep up with them. Blamers come across as incapable of changing as they are stuck in the victim mode.

Some people in the world have the dire need to blame. It is a reflex for them. They just have to blame someone, for them nothing can be an accident or a simple mistake.

Whenever something goes wrong, it has to be a felony. Mistakes are not allowed, whether it be traffic jams, noisy appliances, flight delays, hot summers, cold winters, dry grass, or shedding leaves. Everything is a mistake. Someone must have done something wrong for this to happen, so now here comes the well-deserved whack. We all have met people like these and have been the victim of a blamer. They come in the form of teachers, parents, friends, spouses, etc. These people kill your self-confidence with a single remark, and make healthy people depressed. Their biting remarks and bad mood make your life miserable. Around them, you have to walk on egg shells.

Dealing with a blamer is not easy. They are a type of narcissists (in their own eyes, they can never do anything wrong) with an inflated sense of self. It's very hard to live with a blamer as they always have something hurtful to say, and they truly feel that the fault is external. Most of the times even small interactions with a blamer can leave you feeling awful. It's generally because of their inflated sense of self which shows up in every conversation they have. Their successes and struggles, their own needs are always their top priority, and they don't even realize how they hurt others and make them feel small. The worst part is that if you give them constructive criticism and defend yourself, the problem escalates into a huge fight. It is always their way or the highway. You are left alone to gather yourself in the aftermath of the fight however you can.

So how do you save yourself from a blamer? My advice is to cut cords and distance yourself from such people, if possible. Not just physically, but also emotionally. Don't take their remarks personally. Create boundaries with them physically, emotionally, and mentally. Work double time to build on your confidence and self-esteem. Taking extra self-care would help. And remember to not give them any advice or criticism. .

Blame is a defense strategy we use to avoid self-reflection and ignore the difficult feelings we're going through such as sadness, shame, guilt, or hurt. Blamers don't accept that they are powerless to change others, and continue to blame in the hope that others will change. This learned strategy is the perfect recipe with a great payoff by the means of which we get to be "right, perfect, and justified" in our actions and can preserve our self-esteem. Blamers sit as victims on the stagnated ground of pessimism, helplessness, fury, and aggression. Blamers don't realize that blaming others robs them of many opportunities for self-growth which could, in turn, have helped them develop healthy relationships with themselves and others. Life is challenging not for one, but for all. No one likes to be around a person who either blames himself or others for everything. I understand that we might lose sight and indulge in unmindful ways, like blaming others, to tackle life from time to time, but that shouldn't become a habit.

People with the tendency to self-criticize are mainly those who are taught to focus on their failures by their culture, family, and society. They develop a deep sense of worthlessness. A self-criticizer will sign up for goals beyond their means, and their eventual failure will further deepen their negative feelings of self-blame.

Blaming often leads to –

- Abdication of all responsibilities for thoughts, actions, and words

- Being stuck in the victim mode

- Controlling other's actions and behaviors

- Pessimism and anger

- Lack of compassion and empathy

- Lack of introspection which leads to the halting of self-growth and maturity

- Distorted sense of self

Before I started experimenting with a "new life", I was unaware of why I was blaming others. Often we're so blinded by our everyday existence that it becomes hard to objectively view and accept our own uniqueness and that of others. Like the yin and yang which go hand in hand, and can't exist in isolation, similarly all sides of our personality are also complementary to each other. When we're not balanced, we focus on one side more than on the others. Sometimes, we only want to see our achievements, fame, etc., and forget about our dark side, our ego, selfishness, etc. Other times, we may be too overwhelmed by our dark side and forget the good that exists in us. In reality, we're all unique, and we bring our own flavor to life. Sometimes we forget that fact, and instead of appreciating this uniqueness, we start viewing it as a threat and start blaming it.

This universe operates on the basic principle of cause and effect. Blaming others or yourself blinds you to the underlying causes of an undesirable situation, and makes you shun responsibility for any change you need to make. Without the clear understanding of the underlying cause and effect, you won't know what steps are needed to alleviate the undesirable. So, you end up landing into the same situations over and over again. It's very easy to prove how others screwed up, and build a case against them. It's easy to defend yourself by putting up a fight to prove how you are a victim and are mistreated by others. Screaming, slamming doors, hurting yourself, throwing things are all easy. After such outbursts, you expect the other person to understand, empathize, and apologize for their behavior. You expect them to submit to you with love and care as it is always they who are wrong. If they don't comply, you go into a mad rage again. Such behavior are seen mostly between partners and in parent-child relationships.

I'll give you an example of my client, Rahul. Rahul approached me to get coached about his anger. He was having anger management issues at his workplace and at home. In fact, he had recently had a bitter verbal argument at work in which his boss had to intervene. He was recommended by the Human Resources department to take anger management classes. I know from experience that anger usually has a deep-seated cause, and when Rahul came to me I knew I had to find out what was making him so angry.

During our coaching sessions, I learnt that Rahul had come to the USA from India ten years ago under unique circumstances. He hailed from a family which was once wealthy but had fallen into bad days. His uncle had cheated his father out of his wealth when Rahul was about ten years old. What followed was a litany of court cases that continued to drag on for many decades due to the highly inefficient legal system. His parents faced a lot of anguish in their lives due to their sudden loss of wealth. The uncle was considered as the villain in the family. All their misfortunes seemed to stem from the lack of money for which the uncle was responsible. Blaming the uncle became a common habit in the family, and it was often used as a crutch to hide their own shortcomings and to avoid taking responsibility. When Rahul became older and time came for him to earn a living, he continued with the legacy of blaming his uncle. His real life was supposed to be the so-called "good-life" which was denied to him by his uncle. Like everyone else of his age, he had to work for his living. But in his mind, he was different from others, and anything less than an extraordinary life seemed unfair to him. His dream was to become what his father was in his hay day, a highly successful and respected businessman in the community. Filled with anger for his uncle, he grudgingly decided to move to the States in search of brighter prospects and quick success. However, the last ten years had been by no means easy for him. He lived as a broke student for a number of years, and then found a nine-to-five job. He started making a comfortable living, and had all the material comforts that one could desire. But, to him, life was nowhere close to the good life which should have been rightfully his. In his opinion, he was living a life of compromise, and he was waiting for the day when the court cases would finally be settled in his favor and his real life would begin.

Every aspect of Rahul's conscious experience oozed blame and hatred towards his uncle. All his energy was expended in coming up with ways to resolve the court cases and win the family fortune back. Other times, he would be busy thinking about his potential future once he won the court cases. He was full of anguish and spite, and any minor irritant in his life would end up in a catastrophe. He would not pay attention to the needs of his wife and kids. When his wife interrupted him in his reveries about the court cases, he got excessively angry at his wife. He would lash out at his kids if they consumed too much of his time. He was completely dissatisfied at work. He believed he was meant for big things, and his lowly nine-to-five job was just a temporary fix. He treated his colleagues as peasants, who didn't deserve his respect. As a result, he got embroiled in frequent arguments at work, especially when someone challenged his authority.

During our coaching sessions, it became apparent to me that Rahul was oblivious as to how the blame towards his uncle had affected his entire life. To bring Rahul's attention to the devastating effects of blame in his life, I nudged him with a series of questions. I asked him to consider how life would appear to him if his family had never possessed the wealth in the first place. I asked him to think about all of his life's events and achievements without the lens of that financial loss. I could see a shift in Rahul's body posture and tone once I brought up this topic. There was a hint of pride in his voice as he began to recollect how much he had achieved in his life despite all odds. It was the first time that he had thought about his life in this way, and to his amazement, his life appeared to be littered with success when considered from this angle. It was as if a weight was lifted off his shoulders, and suddenly life looked exciting to him, and not a massive defeat that he was conditioned to suffer since his childhood. Though a sudden realization about life is very powerful in soliciting a change in behavior, however behaviors that are established and reinforced over many years usually take time to change. I advised Rahul to take one step at a time. He had to think about and work on one aspect of his life at a time, starting with his family. We came up with an alternate behavior that he would project towards his family in the future. The subtle changes helped Rahul tremendously to create a better and more fulfilling life for himself and his family. He surprised us all with the consistent and powerful shifts in his life.

I'll give you yet another example of my client Emily to show how blame works in a couple's relationship. Soon after her marriage, the demon of blame reared its ugly head in her relationship with her husband. It all started with her husband finding faults with her for small things. In reality, he was putting the blame for his own challenges on her, so that he didn't have to share his burdens with his family. He didn't want to take responsibility for the situation, and ended up assigning all the blame on her. And, she accepted the blame and stewed in guilt for years, sobbing and crying, until she couldn't take it anymore. Things had come to a point where everything that was going wrong in her husband's life had become her fault. After a couple of anxiety attacks, she gave up and started blaming him back. Then suddenly it became a two-way street, where both of them were blaming each other. This duel lasted for many months until she started considering separation. All she was ready to do at that point was take one last shot at salvaging her marriage.

I coached her to start noting how the actions of people around her were affecting her feelings. She realized that when someone spoke rudely to her or blamed her or gossiped about her, she felt lonely. It affected her self-confidence and self-esteem. In order to lash out, she'd behave the same way with others and hurt them in return. This made her realize that no one wins when we blame; it's a futile exercise with no winners. In any pleasant or unpleasant situation, all the parties involved have some contribution; just one party is never solely responsible. In order to break the chain of blame in her life, I coached her to focus on her own actions and reactions instead of focusing on others. Once she started living with this clarity, she became empowered. She took control of her life, and the blame game stopped having any effect on her.

During our coaching sessions, I asked her to make a list of the common topics that led to fights between her and her husband, and the hurtful behavior that resulted from each such interaction. For each of his actions that would draw her reactions, we made a list of possible constructive counter-behaviors. Using this powerful role-playing technique, I helped her step into her husband's shoes and see him with empathy and compassion. She realized how both of them were merely acting out from their learned behavior. Not knowing what else to do, they did what they knew best; and assigned their hurts and disappointments to each other. With this understanding, she was then able to deal with him gently and kindly. From there on, whenever they were about to engage in an ugly battle, she learnt to retreat, neither accepting any blame on herself, nor blaming him back. After doing this for a month, they both started listening to each other's perspectives with compassion and empathy. Instead of blaming, they began to accept their responsibilities towards themselves and towards each other. They gradually stepped out of the rut of ugly reactions. To put it simply, it really helps to express your feelings in terms of YOURSELF, and not in terms of OTHERS. This alone is immensely helpful in avoiding the trap of the blame game.

A reflective technique that helped me alter my attitude was to observe my emotions which resulted from the behavior of people around me. To help you in the process of removing blame from your life, I urge you to follow the exercises provided below. First of all, find a quiet spot where you won't be distracted for ten minutes at a stretch. Get comfortable in your spot and clear you mind of thoughts and distractions. Create a space for you to be free. Be aware that this is a personal thought exercise, so don't be scared of exploring your feelings. No one has to know what you're thinking.

1. Concentrate on your breathing. Breathe in deeply through your nose and breathe out through our mouth three times. Think about the people in your life or the situations in the last three days that made you feel like a victim. Write down the name of the person and the specific situation that is to blame for an undesirable effect in your life.

____

____

____

2. Recognize the fears, insecurities, shame, and guilt that surround you when you think about this person or situation as in (1). Write these down below.

Fear____

Security_______________________________________

Shame & Guilt________________________________

3. Rub your hands together ten times. Place your writing hand over your heart and say to yourself: "I recognize and accept what I'm going through." I accept my fears, insecurities, shame, and guilt."

4. Now that you have accepted your own fears, insecurities, shame, and guilt, it will be easy for you to look objectively at the situation in (1) again. Write down your reactions, body language, facial expressions, hand gestures, and words when you encountered the person or situation in

(1).

____

____

5. Consider just for the sake of this exercise that you are partly responsible for this situation, or for the person to behave with you this way. I now want you to take a leap of faith and consider that you are fully responsible for your feelings, emotions, fears, insecurities, shame, and guilt that arose as a result of the situation. You are also fully responsible for your language, facial expressions, hand gestures, and words that you used in reaction to these emotions.

6. More likely than not, the emotions that you experienced in the given situation have been there inside you for a long time. This person or situation simply stirred them up and brought them to the surface. Write down other instances where similar emotions arose in you.

Past Situations and People Involved_______________

____

Feelings and Emotions___________________________

____

Actions you Exhibited____________________________

____

Notice how the awareness of your predisposition to these emotions now helps you look at the current situation more objectively.

7. If you feel overwhelmed at this point, it's only natural. Accept yourself as you are with your limitations. When you accept yourself fully, you will be able to act appropriately when a similar situation occurs in your life. Think about the small positive changes that you can bring about in your life without the control and expectation from others. Write down specific changes that you are ready to bring about when similar situations occur again. Even if it is a small change like a positive word or a soft gaze instead of an eye roll, it will go a long way in improving your life.

____

____

____

8. Communicate your feelings to others. Don't keep your one-upman ship as it shows the other person that you're sitting on your pedestal, shunning all your responsibility for changing.

Instead of saying -

You don't love me or you don't care for me or you are a mean person

Try saying –

"I feel sad and angry when you don't give me attention. If

we can spend more quality time with each other, it will help."

Or,

"I feel angry when you don't keep your promise for a date night."

Write down how you would phrase your sentences for the situation if it happens next time. If you have a few of them handy, it'll help you when the situation occurs again.

____

____

____

Congratulations! Now you have the awareness and the tools to manage the blame game in your life.

CHAPTER 3

JUDGE Me Not!

"Thinking is difficult. That's why most people judge." – Carl Jung

Judgment refers to the process of drawing conclusions, based on evidence, to evaluate events and people. Evolution has made humans come up with several mental shortcuts to make snap decisions and preserve energy. One of these shortcuts is making quick judgments. After all, as hunter-gatherers, when we were attacked by predators, it was necessary to make a quick decision to save oneself. Wasting crucial seconds to make elaborate plans when under attack would have meant getting killed. Our lives depended on how quickly we judged the situations and took actions. Though once an effective tool, the innate human habit of making judgments is now highly detrimental under the demands placed by modern society.

The volume of stimuli bombarding our senses has grown tremendously, and it continues to grow at a mind-numbing rate with the advent of social media. In this complex environment, where interpersonal dynamics, societal structure, and work environment are constantly evolving, all of us rely on mental tools that were literally invented during the Stone Age. We make snap judgments about other people and about ourselves based on appearance, race, age, and sexual orientation. We judge others on their actions, terming something ethical or unethical, right or wrong, good or bad. We judge people and societies, terming some as docile vs. aggressive, atheist vs. religious, civilized vs. uncivilized, first world vs. third world. For example, we're all awed by celebrities. In some countries they are even worshiped like God. However like all humans, they may have their own vices or dysfunctional relationships at home. Imagine that while walking on the street you see a man give food to the homeless. Someone may think of him as a noble soul, whereas another may claim that doling out alms to the homeless is encouraging homelessness. Suppose you received a terse response from someone via email or text, so you thought he/she was rude. But in reality, the person might have been in a hurry, and still wanted to ensure that he/she responded to you. Think of a wife who was excited about sharing some news with her husband when he came back from work. But she didn't get the response that she was expecting. Her husband might have had a hard day at work, but she concluded that he was simply not interested, and then their relationship begin to fall apart. We make judgments not only about others, but also about ourselves; about our body shape, success, and intelligence. Either we judge to inflate our sense of self or depreciate ourselves to damage our self-esteem and self-respect.

I'd like to share a funny but pertinent experience from my childhood about being judged. I had grown tall at a young age, and by the time I reached the sixth grade I was already 5'7''. In social gatherings, when people would come to know that I was in grade six, they would instantly ask me how many times I had failed in school. They simply couldn't believe that a twelve-year-old girl could be so tall. Though it looks harmless now, but at that time this really tormented me, and I was extremely shy to meet people socially.

When I was growing up, I thought some of my

classmates as notorious. They were always involved in mischief, and I thought they wouldn't reach anywhere in their lives. Fast forward to twenty years later, and some of these people hold executive positions in large multinational organizations. One of them is a highly successful entrepreneur.

Humans have a strong tendency to make judgments based on their implicit biases. In fact, it's scientifically proven that biases are all-pervasive. We all operate from some degree of bias related to race, color, sex, age, body size, disability, nationality, religion, mannerisms, clothes, accent, and social status. These biases are rooted in family values, social conditioning, and are often percolated through popular culture. Implicit biases are different from explicit biases. With explicit bias, we're aware of our prejudices and attitudes. On the other hand, implicit bias involves all of the subconscious feelings, perceptions, attitudes, and stereotypes that have developed as a result of prior influences and imprints. We can have laws against explicit biases, but implicit biases are very difficult to control. Implicit biases are often so deep-rooted that the person acting out of bias is often ignorant of them. It's usually the person who keeps the bias that pays the highest price. Their sense of reality is forever altered, and all their decisions in life are driven from biased lenses. Whom they befriend, where they go for vacations, what car they drive, the neighborhood they live in, where they work, and other bigger life choices like whom they marry will all be based on their implicit biases. Other forms of judgment are statistically incorrect ways of thinking. Take for instance, you visited a foreign country for the first time and had an unpleasant encounter with a native. You may term all the people in that country as bad. Our brain forces us to think in generalizations, based on sample sizes that may be statistically insignificant. Judgments are also formed as a result of past experiences. Once bitten, twice shy. Consider that you met someone in a social setting who left you with a bad feeling. Maybe he/she was just having a bad day, but based on that one interaction you might end up categorizing other people like him/her in the future. We're all familiar with the phrase "first impression is the last impression". This is especially true for first dates and job interviews.

Judgment is also used as a shield to hide negative feelings about some aspect of our lives and personalities. If we're insecure about ourselves, trashing others who seem better than us makes us feel superior to them. Humans are no different than pack animals. When someone new enters a group, such as a family or a team, it's common for the members of that group to judge the new entrant. If the existing members feel threatened by the new entrant, they start to back bite to ensure that the status of the new member is kept in check. They are trying to spread bad words about the person to prevent him/her from rising above them in the hierarchy. Let me cite a personal example. I got married after a short courtship with my husband, and I had little to no interaction with his family before marriage. After marriage, his family started to judge me on the amount of time I spent talking to them on a daily basis. I came from a family where personal space was respected, and healthy boundaries were maintained. However, my way of functioning was judged to be rude and aloof by my in-laws. They would explicitly show their dissatisfaction to me and my husband. My husband also started judging my behavior as a result. I brought many behavioral changes in my life to make them comfortable, but nothing I did satisfied them. After many years of marriage, I gave up, and judged them for not giving me a safe space to live and exist. I literally stopped speaking to them because no matter what I said and did, I was always misjudged. This led to daily fights in our entire family, and created walls between me and my husband. I realized that judgment can create discord, especially when the relationships within a family are all based on shame and insecurities. Judgment, if not nipped in the bud, has the power to destroy relationships.

Judgment often starts from within, and then becomes the basis for judging others. Each of us has a different bar to measure our own self-worth. It could be based on accolades like success and fame, or attributes like beauty, relationships, intellect, etc. What we use as a measure of our own self-worth becomes the yardstick by which we measure others as well. Our fixation on a specific aspect invariably comes from a past experience where people judged us, usually during growing-up years. In other words, our judgments about others or our own selves are mostly borrowed.

In essence, judging someone or something is to create a hypothesis based on evidence. It is not much different than how scientific theories are hypothesized. The problem is that unlike the formal scientific process, we often make judgments based on insufficient data, merely based on our feelings, and don't test the validity of our hypothesis by subjecting it to rigorous experimentation to see whether they hold true in multiple situations. At the end of the day, all our judgments are mere anecdotal generalizations or mental distractions, without any of them having sufficient logical backing. Judging others negatively creates a bad energy in relationships, resulting in ego tussles, anger, resentment, and revenge. On the other hand, judging someone favorably based on certain traits may blind you to the negative influences they may have in your life. The point I'm trying to make here is that every individual has both strengths and weaknesses on a whole. It's important to realize that any judgment you make is only your interpretation, and not the ultimate truth. There is always a grey area that you haven't fully understood.

The uglier face of judgment can mostly be seen in families. We can choose the friends we keep or where we work, but we can't choose our family. When someone gets judged by their family members, they get a space as big as a "shoe-box" to exist. All the space for them to express, grow, and flourish is destroyed. Self-judgment is also particularly harmful as it clouds your views about your abilities and attributes, limiting what you can achieve in life. A judger will never be able to effectively engage with oneself or with the world.

If only you walk in someone's shoes for a mile, will you understand how life occurs for him, and why he does what he does. This generates a lot of compassion and empathy, and takes you away from judgment. But at the same time, there can't be a judgment-free life. Our mind is constantly collecting information and processing it in subconscious ways, and forming judgments is one of the native functions of the mind to remain active. However, in today's age and time, judgment is no longer a powerful tool, and it creates havoc. When our inner being is balanced, we use our judgment to save ourselves from potentially dangerous situations by making clearer and wiser decisions. But when we use our judgment with an imbalanced and reactive mindset, we start hurting others by pointing fingers and by making others feel inferior to us. Imagine a doctor, teacher, or a therapist who judges their patients or students instead of helping them. Can you imagine the consequences?

I discussed earlier in this chapter how judgment caused a rift in my marital life. I finally worked on my judgments after many years of turmoil. I need not have waited so long. The process looked something like this - a) I realized how powerless we're in changing others in a relationship. b) I accepted all my traits and that of others. This allowed us to have an open and honest communication among ourselves. c) I spoke to everyone vulnerably, in terms of my own feelings. d) I stopped mending myself to fit into the good books of others, and maintained my calm while interacting with them. The key point here is that I chose to indulge in self-care and maintained healthy boundaries. It takes one person to stand up strongly to break the pattern. The next time they judged me and expressed their dissatisfaction explicitly, I didn't take it personally. I reminded them that judgment in our relationship will only drift us apart. I assured them of not having any ill-intent and that they had nothing to be afraid of. After several months of doing this, my relationship with them finally cooled down, and we started to accept each other without judgement.

To help you see where you judge yourself and others, please follow the exercises listed below. First, find a place where you can be comfortable. It can be your favorite couch, your bed, or a coffee shop.

1. Dwelling in the grey area helps us understand that things are not always black and white. We're too quick to judge others and assume the worst in them. Suppose you see someone underdressed or overdressed at a party. You may judge them as rich or as a wannabe, but they might be coming directly from work or from another event. Your judgment may cost you the chance for a good relationship with that person. It is important to understand that we have our own opinions and thoughts, but they are just our perceptions, and not the ultimate truth. Think how often it has happened that you went and watched a movie and said that the movie was bad. In such cases you are merely stating your judgment. And, others decide not to watch the movie based on your judgment. Instead, if you had said that the movie didn't grip me, it would have left others with a chance to explore whether they liked the movie for themselves.

Think about a relationship that is not going well in your life, and write down your thoughts in the space below.

Fear____

____

____

2. Read the thoughts you have written above. Do you see the judgment in them towards yourself and others? Now write down how you are judging yourself and others. What are the trigger points? "Everything that irritates us about others can lead us to an understanding of our self." – Carl Jung

____

____

____

3. The first step to tackle judgment is by accepting the differences, and not just the similarities between you and others. No two humans are ever the same. Even the two sides of your face can never be identical. Even a small step to accept the differences go a long way. Acceptance doesn't mean that you have to change yourself to become like the other person. You can peacefully co-exist with others by merely acknowledging that there are differences. Remember that you always have the free will to do what you are comfortable with without disrespecting others, and so do other people. Live and let live. We don't know what it feels like to walk in someone's shoes and live their lives. Give respect and accept.

____

____

____

Self-love and acceptance: Write down the areas that you are not accepting and loving about yourself.

____

____

____

The more you accept and love yourself, the easier it will be for you to accept the differences in others. Think about the differences that you have with the person in (1). What are the differences you can accept about them?

Differences_____________________________

____

____

4. Most of the times we perceive other's actions or words through our own biases. We're merely reacting to others from a superficial understanding of their tone, choice of words, or actions. When you listen to the other person with compassion, empathy, and by being fully present (in body and mind) in the moment, you will start to understand what they truly want to say to you. This will prevent you from jumping to not into conclusions and making judgments. Ask questions to gather more understanding rather than passing judgments too quickly.

5. Pause is the keyword for people who are willing to remove the barricade of their judgment. This means before you speak out of your judgment impulsively, take a pause. This will help you stay curious about the grey area before you jump on to judge others. In this way, you opinionate less and create less differences. Speak up only when you're offering any real help or valuable input, otherwise take a pause. Think of the areas where you can take a pause next time, and write them down.

____

____

____

You will be amazed to realize how much vastness we carry inside us that can be expanded to accept people with their differences and love them. The less you judge others the more you set yourself free from the shackles of expectations. You discover freedom.

"Love is the absence of judgment." – Dalai Lama

CHAPTER 4

Negative Thinking!

"Negativity is like burning plastic: while destroying itself, it annoys everyone with its stench."

— Charbel Tadros

Whether we like to acknowledge it or not, we're what we think. Our minds and bodies are far more interconnected than we realize. People who have practiced yoga can easily relate to this fact – you simply fall out of the yoga pose if your mind diverts. I remember an incident when I met a friend after completing a ten-day self-help course. She kept asking me if I had undergone some beauty treatments on my face since my skin was visibly radiant and softer. In reality, all I had done during that time was to rid my mind of many negative thoughts, and that serenity was what was being reflected by my body. It is seen commonly that people with unresolved issues and negative thinking reflect the same through heavy and stiff bodies and long faces. We all have someone in our lives to whom we can attribute these traits; even worse, that person can even be us. Seeing the glass as "half-full" or "half-empty" is a choice that we have to make at every step of our lives, and that eventually shapes our personalities.

Even though in this chapter I'm talking about negative thinking, it's important to note that fixation on anything "highly positive" or "highly negative" has dire consequences. For instance, there are two people, A and B, who want to rent a showroom for their furniture business. Mr. A is a joyous person, who loves to initiate new projects. His mind is always teeming with the possibilities any opportunity presents. There isn't a single sad or negative bone in his body. However due to his overoptimistic approach he usually ignores the risks or the limiting aspects of things. When Mr. A got to know about the showroom, he could visualize how he could convert that space into a national chain. And, he immediately signed a five-year lease. This turned out be a foolhardy investment as he didn't factor in the other risks before jumping on this opportunity. On the other hand, Mr. B is a tense person, who looks at limitations more than the opportunities available in any scenario. In this situation, he let go of the showroom as he had scrutinized all the risks involved with a magnifying glass. That made him extremely wary, and he walked away from the deal. Both A and B, in this scenario, didn't fully analyze their resources and limitations, and lost the opportunity that knocked on their doors.

I'd like to share the story of one of my clients here who had come to me to resolve his relationship issues with his wife. He described how his wife didn't understand him, and was demanding, that she constantly nagged him and made him do things he didn't like. He thought he should have dated her a little longer before marrying her so that he could have realized her true personality. When he saw his friends living happily with their wives, he envied them, and resented his wife for not giving him the same experience. He insisted that I speak to his wife and fix her. He was convinced that all their problems stemmed from her. During our sessions, he moaned about how he always met the wrong people. When I probed him a little more about his past, he revealed how his life had never worked out for him.

His childhood was a mess because his parents didn't have enough money, and he never had the same opportunities as some of his other friends. His parents were busy fighting among themselves and were never emotionally available to him. His teachers had been unfair to him and didn't give him good grades because he was a stutterer, and because of that he couldn't attend his dream college. His girlfriend was disloyal to him and left him for his friend. He never got the job he deserved, and his professional career wasn't where it should have been. After listening to his stories for hours, I asked him how often he felt like this. In keeping with my expectation, he said that this was his life. When I asked him to name one thing for which he was thankful in his life, he couldn't think of anything. To him life was genuinely a trouble. I challenged him to come up with at least one thing that was working for him. I nudged him to see that he, at least, had food to eat, clothes to wear, a healthy body, and a shelter. After much persuasion, he agreed that his life had afforded him some good things after all. I suggested him a couple of solutions which he practiced for the next few weeks (I have listed those solutions at the end of this chapter). That made him have an "ah ha" moment where he realized that his wife was not the source of his problems. Rather, it was his own negative thinking that had been impacting his entire life. We could track his negative attitude back to his parents, and realized that it was learned behavior. He realized that since his childhood, he had a habit of dramatizing and outsourcing the source of problems so that he could look good in front of other people. Instead of taking responsibility of changing per the situation, he would expect other people to change, so that his dream life could magically present itself. Whenever he saw glimpses of the positives in his life, and realized that his baggage of negativity was unnecessary, he would become anxious. His brain would kick in and force him to look at all the negatives again and again. His mind would present logic after logic about how his life was so stressful. As negative thinking is a learned behavior, it fights back with a vengeance when challenged. I suggested him to wear his favorite-colored wrist band to remind himself about the positive side of his life.

Can't we all relate to these traits in one way or another?

Most of us obsess over what may go wrong instead of what may go right, what is going wrong instead of what is going right, or what went wrong instead of what went right. Negativity is not just in our minds. It shows up in our body postures, our choice of words, the music we listen to, the clothes we wear, our recreational activities, the types of friends we hang out with, the food we eat, and other life choices. Negative-thinkers can't be creators, as they are busy second guessing themselves - their luck, bodies, abilities, or situations. They usually view the world as a zero-sum game where there are clear winners and losers. Overly competitive, they usually put down others who are not as successful as they are. In short, negativity leads to negative feelings and behaviors which are destructive, un-cooperative, pessimistic, and unhealthy. Negative-thinkers don't realize their own folly and consider themselves to be the victims of external factors. It could be the fault of their parents, partners, upbringing, situations, or the world at large. Negative-thinkers follow one of the two predictable paths. They may either go into their shell of solitude, crankiness, and grouchy behavior. Or they may become overly aggressive, snap back at the slightest of provocations, and become trigger happy. People with a negative mindset survive and thrive on manufactured stress. They feel as if stress is all around them, but most of it is usually self-inflicted. They like to be in the company of people with similar attitudes, who validate their ways of thinking. They turn light-hearted moments into gloom and doom. It starts small but slowly becomes a self-destructive habit.

I firmly believe that we're the reflections of the environments in which we were raised. If that environment was filled with negativity, cribbing, crying, verbal or physical abuse, we're naturally inclined to carry the same behavior patterns and attitudes. In short, negativity is a like a genetic disorder which runs in families. A major cause of negative thinking is comparison. We've all been socially conditioned to compare ourselves to others. We treat ourselves and others as commodities made of homogeneous attributes that can be compared at every turn. It starts from our childhoods when our parents compare us to our siblings and other kids. Even if they don't say anything explicitly, the subtle differences in how they treat you and those favored kids can say it all. Later we take this mindset to our schools, and compare ourselves to our peers. Slowly, it becomes a part of our operating systems. This unhealthy comparison makes us believe that we're not worthy until we defeat everyone around us and conquer the throne. We turn this world into a battleground rather than into a place where we can learn, grow, and thrive. This habit of comparing can ruin our chances of fostering any meaningful relationships with others. When someone is out there to get you, out do you at every step, the feeling generated is not of warmth or friendship, but of defense and enmity. A person who is always comparing himself with others carries a tremendous amount of stress in everyday life. Instead of focusing on what works in their lives, they are too focused on showing the world how they are better than everyone else around them. A recent upswing in this kind of behavior is seen on social media. How we eat, sleep, celebrate occasions, and take vacations, is all up for display, and has become potential areas for comparison between people, whether they know each other personally or not.

Negativity also stems for being too attached to a certain outcome in our lives, even though some situations do call for such neediness. For example, a sole breadwinner in the family is hoping to get a raise to send her kid to college, a patient awaiting test results after a long and painful medical treatment, a jobless person wanting a job to pay his rent, a student not getting a passing score to get into college, etc. However we often end up bringing the same gravity into our regular lives, where it becomes important to win a conversation, to become more successful than our peers, to get a date with someone of interest, or to see our favorite sports team win a match. We end up treating these situations as if it's life or death even though they are inconsequential to our existence. When we treat everything with this doomsday attitude, we lose sight of what is truly important for us, and we end up making wrong decisions in our lives.

Our beliefs which make us think about "should" or "must" also contribute towards negative thinking. These usually come from inherited family values, culture, and environment. He "should have not" spoken like this at a party, a man "must" be strong and not emotional, women "should" be nurturing and soft-spoken, you "should have" called my mother even if she is mean to you, you "must" apologize to your elders, we "should" attend church every Sunday, etc. These "should" or "must" beliefs constrain us into fixed ways of being, and confine us to a particular way of thinking. People with this attitude often foster fear of failure which prevents them from taking chances in their lives. Each human being is different, with a different perspective on life. Being tied to these ideas makes us feel claustrophobic, where our creativity and expression is stifled, leading to resentment and negative feelings for people who impose these beliefs on us. Another classic example of negative thinking is the "all or nothing attitude", where there are no shades of grey. If we're not selected in a job interview, we feel incompetent and believe that we won't ever be selected for another job. If we're turned down for a date, we feel we're not worthy of love, and are hesitant to approach someone else the next time. If I'm not the richest person in my group, I can't be happy.

All of these might seem obvious in concept, but how many of us truly understand how much destruction this is causing in our lives? Negative thinking is devastating and often leads to the following:

- Anger problems: When your mind is already full of negative thoughts, even the distant noise of a baby crying or the honk of a car on the road can make you burst out in anger and lash out at others.

- Relationships with yourself and others suffer

- Lack of appreciation towards yourself and others

- Health issues: High blood pressure, heart diseases, pains and aches, anxiety, depression

- Not being able to use your opportunities and resources. If you're dwelling on what you don't have, you're blinded to what you do have.

- You'll never be in the present; you're either stuck in the past or dwelling on the future.

We live in uncertain worlds where outcomes are dependent on a multitude of factors which are not necessarily in our control. Over the course of our lives many events occur that might be or might not be up to our expectations. But the thing to note here is that we're never stuck. We can always free ourselves when we truly choose to. Rome was not built in a day, and similarly it takes effort and practice to develop a positive mindset. If you see clearly that you are stuck in a negative thought pattern, you can certainly come out it. However it requires commitment to make the attitude and behavioral shifts. Unfortunately there is no miraculous cure.

All it will take is five minutes every day for the next three-five days to help you see how you're stuck in a negative thought cycle. Before you go to bed, find a comfortable spot and breathe deeply to clear your mind.

1. Think about how your day started. What were your predominant thoughts when you were going about your day? During the rigmarole of the day, it's easy to lose track of your thoughts. An easy way to connect to yourself is to rewind the tape and evaluate all that you have been thinking of that day. Better yet, write down your thoughts every couple of hours in a journal. It will give you a record of your thoughts over a period of time. Out of these thoughts, segregate which were negative and which were positive.

2. Sometimes it's not easy for us to see through our own thoughts. A way to uncover your negative thoughts is to think about the times when you acted negatively. For example, when you used foul language, got angry at someone, got into a fight with others, acted out of competition, etc.

3. After three-five days when you will look at your journal again, it will automatically generate awareness about your thoughts. You will realize that your negative thoughts are generally about the past or the future. For example, my partner will always take me for granted; I will never have enough money to pay my bills; My childhood was much happier than my present; etc. Do you now realize that these negative thoughts are cyclical that don't let you see anything new?

4. Ask yourself what you are losing and what you are gaining by going through the same thought process? We feel that we will find the solution to our problems by repeatedly thinking about them. But "We can't solve problems by using the same kind of thinking we used when we created them." – Albert Einstein

A few techniques to break the pattern of negative thinking are:

a. **Detachment** from your thoughts. Take five minutes in the morning, afternoon, and evening to focus on your breath. Observe the flow of thoughts as they come and go. If you find yourself getting gripped by a thought, remind yourself to focus on your breath. Let your thoughts flow like water. Notice that some thoughts will keep coming back no matter how hard you try to shake them off. Pick up such a thought even when you try to focus on your breath.

➥ _Accept_ the fear, insecurity, or an incident which is underpinning the thought. Breathe in and out ten times and affirm in your mind, "I accept my fears, insecurities, and the particular incident."

➥ To move on from the fear, insecurity, or the incident that is gripping you

- Ask yourself what are the positive learnings from this.

- Think about what new skills you need to acquire. Or what behaviors you need to adopt to cope with a similar situation if it occurs in the future.

Remember, you are always capable of learning new skills, abilities, and behaviors to help you get through any situation. The more you get equipped to deal with a situation, the less fears you will have about it. There was a person who used to make me feel very anxious. I'd continuously fear our next meeting. My insecurities gripped me so strongly that I'd be caught up in negative thoughts for hours, and pray that the person would change. My fears were driven by my inability to deal with this person. When I finally realized that there was a way I could stop that person from controlling me like that, I stopped being negative. When you move the focus from your negative thinking and your fears, and on to the actions you can take, you won't be gripped by negativity anymore. Keeping the focus on your strengths, working on your limitations, inculcating a new behavior, seeking help form others will all help you feel empowered in life. Be the change you wish to create.

➡ Name your negative thoughts. Give a "funny name" to the broad pattern of thinking; it could be about anything: money, appearances, etc. Whenever you detect a string of thought which belongs to the broad thought pattern, you will be reminded of the funny name. This will make it easier for you to let go of the negative thoughts. It could be a simple name like Timmy. And when you find yourself thinking, "You can't do that," or "You're not good enough," you can just yell in your head, "Go away, Timmy! Not today, I'm busy!"

➡ Pick up three sources of negativity. It could be the people around you, the media, or a particular situation. It would help if you can either eliminate them from your life completely or reduce the amount of time you spend with them. While you're developing your positive thinking, it's important to surround yourself with people who are positive and joyous. It could be that you don't have such people in your life currently, but you always have the option to look for them. If you reach out to your church, attend meet-ups, mingle with your colleagues, you will realize that such people are at arm's length; it's just that you didn't notice them earlier. At the same time, try to disconnect from negative people as much as possible.

➡ Stop making mountains out of mole hills. It's better to understand that not every negative thought is doomsday. It's very destructive for your psyche, health, wealth, and relationships. It repels people.

a. A very important practice for everyone, and mostly for negative thinkers, is **gratitude**. Especially when negative thoughts drown you, keep this tool handy to break the pattern. Think of the good things you have in your life such as health, food, shelter, clothes, partner, children, family, and friends. It will make you realize how blessed you already are.

b. Get some **reminder accessories** like stickers, fridge magnets, bookmarks, and jewelry with customized messages that resonate best with you. For example, "Stay Positive", "Gratitude", and "Laughter". Keep it around the area where you spend the maximum amount of time.

The above techniques will help you look back at your past without anger, remorse, and victimization. This is critical for you to shatter the old lenses of fear, insecurity, and a lack mentality. You will stop acting out of the primitive "fight or flight response", and learn to question, "Why am I thinking like this?"

CHAPTER 5

Erase SELF DOUBT!

"**D**oubt kills more dreams than failure ever will."— Suzy Kassem

What is self-doubt? It is the "I can't do it" feeling that arises in us when we're faced with a difficult situation. All of us have experienced butterflies in the stomach before embarking on something important, like a job interview, the first day at college, the first date, getting married, etc. While a little bit of nervous energy is important to keep us on our toes, but self-doubt can be debilitating and can hinder our performance. Imagine that you were offered a new assignment by your boss, because he thought you were the most capable. Instead of feeling motivated, you get filled with self-doubt and worry about your ability to complete the task and how you'd make a joke of yourself in front of your colleagues if you fail. How many of us can see ourselves in this example?

With self-doubt, we kill the creative power present in us. What if Thomas Edison had given up inventing the light bulb after initial failures? What if the Wright Brothers gave up on their dream of flying after crashing innumerable times? Self-doubt always makes us feel like there are heavy rocks tied to our feet, and that we're sinking in deep water, struggling for breath. We quickly make an excuse to get out of that uneasy situation. We run to people around us to ask for their suggestions, taking refuge in their decisions. These heavy rocks pulling us down are our fears of failure, performance anxiety, low self-esteem, feeling of unworthiness, and past traumatic experiences. Most often we're oblivious to the existence of these feelings inside us;

it's just an uneasy feeling that keeps nagging us, and that we think is natural.

What a mess I've made! I should never do anything on my own. I made a fool of myself. I'm not good enough to take a chance. Let me find someone to guide me through this. I'm not experienced enough to even apply for this. These voices are present in all of us. The difference is that some people know how to mute them, whereas some give in to these voices and stay tangled in self-doubt. Speaking of which, I have fallen victim to the same. *Who am I to write this book? I don't have a creative flair. I haven't undergone a course on how to write. So much stuff is available on the internet, why will anyone buy my book? How will I market my book anyways? Where's the network? What will people think of me? What if people judge me and I lose close relationships? Oh man, what a bad idea! I should know my limits. What a fool I'm about to make of myself.* And, with all this going on in my mind I dropped the idea of writing this book three years ago. It seemed like a logical decision back then, but little did I know that I was just giving into my self-doubt.

I had a client who was fired from two jobs successively. The experience paralyzed him with self-doubt. He doubted himself so much that he couldn't apply for another job for six months. I had a friend who had just come out of an abusive relationship. Her previous relationship had also ended on a bitter note when she had found out that her boyfriend had been cheating on her. After her second failed relationship she lost the confidence to choose another partner. She refrained from committing to anyone else for the fear of repeating the same experiences.

When we're afraid to act, we end up making excuses to put it off indefinitely. Procrastination is usually the first symptom of self-doubt. It leads us to make excuses to avoid venturing out of our comfort zones. Some common thoughts may be: I may never be able to succeed as I don't have that high-flying degree; I'm happy in an abusive relationship because I'm not sure if I'll find another partner, etc. Self-doubt is the enemy of creation, and prevents us from thinking creatively and out-of-the-box. We're at our creative and productive best only when we're comfortable and are operating in our element. People operating from self-doubt tend to set the ground for future failures, and make negative conclusions about their lives, which become artificial barriers for them. If I'm born in poverty, I believe that all odds are stacked up against me, and I can never be rich. This thought now becomes a barrier for me.

One of the main causes for self-doubt is underwhelming beliefs about oneself which might be inherited from our families. If our parents didn't trust themselves, and let their parents and friends make all their decisions for them, they wouldn't know how to let us make ours. During childhood it's important to learn how to make decisions. Children from a young age need to be encouraged to make decisions about their own food, toys, clothes, friends, time management, and studies. If in our childhood, we're not allowed to make these decisions, we will lack self-awareness, and will be riddled with self-doubt all our lives. In many cultures even the choice of partner is made by the parents. The child is made to rely on the parents for all their decisions. Even if the child chooses a partner, they need to get their parents' approval about it. This is the height of self-doubt. It's a fact that we choose like-minded people in our lives. Birds of the same feather flock together. If you're riddled with self-doubt, you will invariably end up choosing similar people in your life, and the more you're surrounded with such negative people, the harder will it be for you to break the shackles and think differently.

Comparison with others is also a big reason due to which self-doubt can creep into our minds. But we should never compare ourselves with others. It takes a number of factors, known or hidden, to come into play for things to happen the way they do. When we compare, we end up looking at all our deficiencies. And, these deficiencies seem like the obvious reasons for our failures. It is very important to introspect and grow from the point at which we're in our life's journey. Comparing ourselves with others will only exacerbate the feeling of lack, and make us doubt our abilities. People who compare themselves with others care too much about what others think about them. This feeling is paralyzing, and instead of doing the things that are meaningful for us at the current moment, we end up running after shiny objects that somebody else might possess. When we compare ourselves to others and fall short, we end up faking our own lives. We become so good at faking that we forget what we really need to work on. The philosophy of "fake it till you make it" may not lead you anywhere.

Underestimating our self, not owning up to our

strengths and weaknesses, are all sure ways of feeling incompetent. How many times have we attributed our success to fluke? We're too fixated on what we don't have, and end up devaluing what we do have. Many a times we're not even fully aware of our strengths, and we start to doubt ourselves. Setting unrealistic goals is also a way to feel defeated which again leads to self-doubt. While it may be important to challenge ourselves at times by setting goals that stretch us, but habitually setting impossible goals makes us feel like a loser, and we start to doubt about abilities to succeed. The only thing we can do is give our best shot, and remember that the final outcome may or may not be at par with our expectations. Most of the learning happens after the incident occurs. Learn from your experiences, recalibrate, and try again. You already have what it takes.

I was working with one of my clients who was about forty. When it came to the point where he had to make a decision about his work, he got cold feet. He felt the need to run and ask his close confidants if he was making the right decision. This was an eye opening moment for us. We realized how much self-doubt he had even in his advanced age. He was still making his decisions based on the advice from his acquaintances. He was making excuses for not doing what was expected of him, and was completely unapologetic about it. He tried to give self-justification for why he couldn't, shouldn't, or won't do what was needed to be done. At work he was not able to take decisions, and constantly passed on the buck to others. This was causing him to fall behind in his projects. Excuses and procrastination were holding him back.

In order to rid him of self-doubt, we got him to acknowledge his excuses and how that was affecting him. We began by making him take small evaluative decisions. This helped him learn how to take responsibility for his decisions. He eventually discovered himself, and started realizing his strengths and weaknesses. He enhanced his strengths and worked on his limitations. He started to learn the skill of decision-making and avoiding self-doubt. This means that he learnt how not to loathe himself when his decisions didn't yield the desired outcomes, and instead how to look at it as a lesson for the future. It is only when we cross the threshold of the unknown that we start learning and growing as individuals. Self-doubt prevents us from crossing that threshold, and makes us operate ineffectively in the face of ambiguity.

These days there is a twisted sense of confidence that is being propagated in our culture. People seem to put their focus on their appearances rather than on truly believing in themselves and a higher power. There are standards to be met in every aspect from the clothes we wear to how we speak and how much money we earn, and that leads to confidence now. When I made the shift from acting confident to truly feeling confident, my self-doubt issues started to resolve. There will always be things that I know, and those that I don't. But if I sit back in the fear of unknown then I will never be able to learn and grow. None of us are born with skills, we acquire them over the course of our lives. The capacity to learn new skills is innate in humans. Our brains are hardwired to learn from others and from our surroundings. It's just the way we're built through evolution. The speed at which we inculcate these skills may differ from person to person. Nevertheless, all of us possess the mental faculties to learn and grow. Self-doubt is questioning this innate ability that makes you human. However, everyone has their own definition of confidence. We feel that we need to acquire material possessions in order to feel confident. Money, fame, power, and a perfect body are all status symbols now. We have been told by our culture that we can be confident only when we have the above. And, we start running on the hamster wheel with all our might, day and night, trying to get to the top. But even when we reach there, we don't stop because it never fills the hole created in us by our self-doubt. We need to acquire more, more, and more, and this cycle never stops. All of us already have "all that it takes" to run our lives. The biggest tool available to human beings is their ability to assimilate, learn, and grow. Faith in this ability gives us the confidence to trust the process of life. When the trust is greater than the fears, we feel confident. We can't make sense of it before we start doing it. At the same time, it is important to understand that each of us is gifted uniquely. Not everyone will have the same talents, and it would be foolish to chase after everything in life!

Self-doubt is all in the mind. It generally has little to no existence in the real world. Because we're thinking fearfully, we end up not living our lives confidently. The exercises below will help you understand your tendency to self-doubt.

1. List some areas from your past or in the present

where you were/are stuck in self-doubt.

____

____

____

2. From the above list, choose one of the areas that you would like to work on. Introspect on the genesis of your self-doubt in this area. To help you navigate through this step, I have listed four prominent reasons for self-doubt.

Fear of the unknown: While it is completely normal to be anxious when embarking on something new, self-doubt stops you from even trying.

Fear of failure: Being too attached to the outcome makes you fear failure. It would mean lowering yourself in your own eyes and fearing being ousted from the group.

Comparison: When you're concerned about how you would fare in comparison to others, you begin to doubt your abilities and actions. Comparison is futile; even the fingerprints on both your hands are different.

Lack of responsibility: You never learnt the process of decision-making and taking responsibility since childhood. Your caretakers may have been poor role models who never took responsibility for themselves. Or they never let you make your own decisions, leaving you with a feeling of incompetence.

Fear of the unknown

____

Fear of failure

____

Comparison

____

Lack of responsibility

____

3. Now that you know how self-doubt works in you, you need to learn how to believe in yourself.

a. Be your own "decision-maker". Only you know yourself and what works best for you. No one knows you better than you. It's okay to ask for suggestion from others, but their approval is not the last word.

b. Plan your next step of action.

c. Learn from the fall out.

d. Don't worry about what others may think. Others have enough baggage of their own, and don't have the time to dwell on your life.

e. Positive self-talk

f. Plan the next steps again.

g. Learn from your fall out.

h. Change your direction based on your new learning.

i. Celebrate your small wins.

j. Little by little you start believing in yourself.

"Stop procrastination. Take action!"

CHAPTER 6

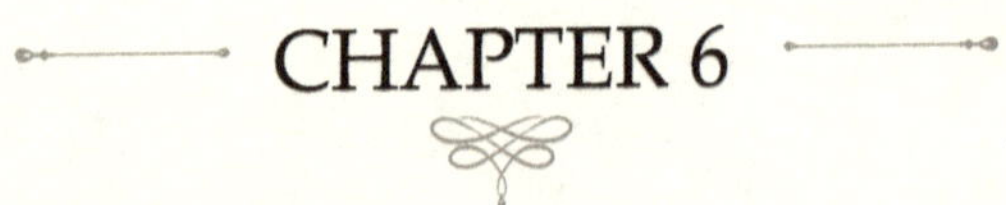

Banish INSECURITY to Let in Security!

**"Insecurity is a lie someone told you about yourself."
- Unknown**

Insecurity can be simply put as not feeling secure in one or more areas of your life. Humans are social animals who are highly interdependent on each other. Insecurity usually has hidden in its core a belief: I'm fat, I'm ugly, I lack intelligence, I'm poor, so on and so forth. This makes us feel inept to deal with challenges, and makes us feel small in comparison to others. If you think that you're ugly or fat, how do you feel about approaching an attractive person of the opposite sex? If you feel you're not successful in your career, how do you feel in the company of highly accomplished people? If you think you're not interesting, how do you feel when you're talking to an all-rounder? If you've had any of these experiences, you're not alone. Most of us grapple with some form of insecurity or the other. Insecurity is part of the human condition, hardwired into our very brains by the process of evolution. In the hunter-gatherer days, it was life threatening to be ousted from a group since people needed the protection and resources of a tribe to survive. We're social animals, and we're afraid of being left alone. Even though, in the modern world, we don't rely on people the same way anymore, but everyday situations still elicit the same biochemical responses in our brains. Our insecurities show up at different degrees in various settings – with our parents, siblings, friends, partners, or children. While it may not be possible to completely rid the brain of reactions that causes insecurity, we can certainly learn how to deal with it strongly.

I can think of a personal example from my life to illustrate this. When I was in the fourth grade, I had a teacher who for no reason would pick on me in front of the whole class. During summer breaks, we were told to read our entire English books and write the meanings of difficult words. In every class she would make it a point to single me out. She would make me say the meanings of difficult words one after the other till I finally got one wrong. After that she would humiliate me in front of the whole class. This continued for a good three years, and during this time I wasn't even aware of how this was affecting me. By the time I was in the sixth grade, I had lost interest in studies. I had gone into my shell, and I was a complete introvert at school. I was so scared to go to school that once I pretended to have a stomachache for a week. Finally when my mom took me to the doctor, I was busted. When my mother asked for an explanation, I told her I was afraid of my teachers and that no one liked me at school. She got worried, and on further investigation she realized to her horror how I was being bullied, not by other kids, but by my own teacher. But by that time it was too late. The hurt had got too deeply ingrained in my psyche. I was ashamed of myself, and I tried too hard to please others. I was numb, lost, and confused. On seeing my misery, my mother made me change my school. My new school was very uplifting. My teachers and classmates were very welcoming, loving, and friendly. Slowly I grew out of my pain, and by the time I graduated from high school, I had many friends, and I was a successful student. It was not until I started meditating that I realized I still had insecurities in me. I'm not good enough, this was something I still felt deep down. And, this was still affecting me at a professional and personal level.

As already discussed, insecurity is a part of our genetic makeup. Our bodies produce the chemicals which help us survive perceived threats by fight, flight, or freeze reactions. We all have the propensity to feel insecure, but the degree of it differs from person to person. Though we're all insecure, some are more so than others.

Any kind of insecurity mostly generates the fear of being left out or getting rejected. If we've experienced this in the past, we're terrified that this would happen in our present as well. The feeling of being unloved and unaccepted continuously burns our self-esteem and self-worth into ashes. Before somebody rejects us, we reject ourselves. We choose to remain reticent towards our partners, loved ones, or other people who matter to us. We use different defense mechanisms to deal with our fear of being rejected. Some may retreat into their shells and refuse to participate in social settings. Others may overcompensate this fear by trying too hard, whether at work or at relationships. We don't realize that this is not a solution, but a temporary fix. This allows the insecurity to feed on itself, letting it grow bigger and bigger each time something goes wrong. Take for instance Nick. When he was eight years old, he had gone shopping for clothes with his parents. His parents made faces and remarked on his choice of clothes. This was not the first time he was being rejected by his parents, but this incident served to drive the nail in the coffin. Ever since that incident he stopped sharing his thoughts and likings with others under the fear of rejection. Nick is now thirty-five years of age, but still feels a strong fear of rejection which affects his relationship with his wife, peers, and colleagues. All his decisions in life have been taken to please others, and this has been very damaging for his life. Since he fears to express himself, he feels misunderstood, lacks intimacy with others, and feels lonely. This insecurity generates behavior and actions which create more reasons for his fear to increase. However for Nick, his experience is traumatic, and he can't see through this fog to detect the insecurity eating him from inside.

Insecure feelings about oneself can be a big obstacle in life. The first casualty is usually the ability to forge healthy relationships with parents, partners, or kids. If we think our parents favor our sibling more, we might try too hard to prove ourselves worthy of their love and approval. We develop an unhealthy competition with our sibling which might last for a lifetime. In every dining table conversation, we might try to best our sibling. We might even try to sabotage our sibling's success in a misguided attempt to gain our parents' favor. Say if Max is insecure about his financial status, he will take his wife's remarks on this topic, however small, to heart. He might lash out at his wife, and won't be able to have an open and fulfilling relationship with her. Suppose Judy has body image issues, and is insecure about her looks. She is continuously looking out for signs that her boyfriend might leave her for someone prettier. As a result she is over-possessive and over-bearing. Men who are insecure about their masculinity are often afraid to express their emotions to their partners and kids, and are generally not susceptible to their wives' influence. Insecurity makes us defensive and doesn't let us be vulnerable with people around us. Openness, honesty, and vulnerability are the pillars on which our relationships thrive. Without these traits, we can never have secure and trusting relationships. An insecure person is constantly looking out for validation from the world around them, and when they are unable to get the validation they desire, they start to behave awkwardly as if there has been a short circuit in their brains. Such people may become overly intrusive and heavy-handed with their kids, abusive towards their partners, employees, and even pets. This is classic narcissist-type behavior where one starts to inflate their sense of self and disassociates with their shortcomings. Parents with this syndrome start to draw a sense of personal success from the achievement of their kids.

Many studies show that insecurity is toxic for all relationships. An unhealthy parent-child relationship, where parents don't place trust on the child, plants insecurity in the child's mind. Later as an adult, this person will bring trust issues in his relationship with his partner. He will always be looking at his partner with suspicion. He will never be able to forge a close, trusting, interdependent, and intimate partnership. He will be overly guarded about himself and won't risk vulnerability. This kind of a person will try to defend himself and show hostility at the slightest provocation. They're aggressive not because they are mean, but because everything seems like a threat to them. Or such a person may also become overly needy. They will develop attention-seeking behavior, and will fish for compliments all the time. They will need constant validation to feel good about themselves.

There are many researches that show a direct link between self-confidence and success. Self-confidence by itself means that you're secure about yourself. On the other hand, insecurity is the opposite of self-confidence. Suppose Timothy was a young professional who had recently joined a banking firm. He was the youngest team member, and all the other people had, at least, five more years of experience than him. Timothy was insecure about his abilities in spite of having all the credentials. He was an MBA from a reputable university, and had already worked in a couple of industries. But his insecurity came from his childhood experiences where his parents favored his overachieving sibling more than him. Timothy felt he was not "good enough" to be loved and accepted. He convinced himself to play second fiddle in all spheres of life, and became a people-pleaser. He would feel very nervous and anxious around others. However ill-founded they may have been, his insecurities were real to him. Even though he had performed well in his job interviews, he suspected that he had been hired on a fluke. Due to his insecure nature he was indecisive and couldn't make his own decisions. He would rely on his colleagues to make every decision about projects. He would suck up to his colleagues and seniors to stay in their good books. He was under confident about his ideas, and was shy to present them in team meetings. Due to his toxic lack of self-belief he was very stressed at work, and every day seemed like a battle to him. He felt like an imposter, and was constantly on the lookout for approaching disaster. But actually Timothy had much to offer to his team; it's just that he couldn't see his good qualities as he was so fixated on his shortcomings. As a result, success seemed like a distant thing to him.

Insecurity leads to mental health conditions such as narcissism, anxiety, depression, sleep disorders, mood swings, and paranoia. It also leads to poor lifestyle choices like addiction and bad eating habits which can cause weight gain and many other physiological problems like hypertension, diabetes, heart disease, etc.

Our childhood experiences play a big part in shaping who we are. Any trauma, wound, or abandonment issue can lead us to feel insecure about ourselves in many ways. This shapes our beliefs for the rest of our lives.

- A caregiver may unconsciously belittle a child's choices, expressions, or traits. This may cause the child to believe that he or she is not good enough. A father may think that ballet is too feminine, and may discourage his son from taking it up even if he's good at it. A child may not be allowed to express himself or herself through their choices.

- Often adults can objectify children. They may label them as cute or innocent, and even use mocking language that they would for a toy or a pet. By doing so they fail to consider the child's emotions. This makes the child feel judged and inferior, as if his feelings don't matter.

- Parents may reprimand their kids mindlessly by

saying things like: "How dumb of you!"; "You couldn't understand such a simple thing!"; "Stupid!" This makes the child feel humiliated and incompetent, and he might grow up to be an under confident, inexpressive adult.

- Some parents may praise their children too much for their successes or achievements, and not for their personal traits. Such children may grow up to be individuals who drive their sense of self from achievements and compliments. As emotions were never important, they will become worldly, dispassionate, and cold. Such people will be highly competitive, jealous, and hyper-vigilant. They will also bring the same baggage in their relationships.

- Some parents may shower exaggerated and insincere praises on their kids. This is equally bad for the kid's psychology. They can see through the façade and think that they lack something which needs hiding or fixing. To a child, this invariably feels like rejection. On the flip side, the kid might get a false sense of self and become a braggart.

- There may be times when the parents are too engrossed with their own lives, and may not pick up signs of distress in their child. Even if the child does express her emotions, the parents may not register the gravity of the situation and shun/belittle/ignore/criticize their thoughts and emotions. This will generate feelings of loneliness and abandonment in the child, and she will carry the same emotions for her partners and children when she grows up.

- Those parents who don't respect the boundaries of their kids, and are overly intrusive in their lives don't let the kids learn how to make their own decisions. Their kids will be full of self-doubt, lack self-reliance, will not know how to trust themselves and others, and will develop multiple insecurities, and will become introverts.

- Parents can also pass on their own insecurities to their children through their behavior and language. Their insecurities about money, education, social standing, appearance, luck, etc. might pass on to the children. Similar types of insecurities runs in families, and create the same types of blocks in the lives of successive generations.

Lack of protection from care givers → Insecurity seeps in → Low self-esteem → Lack of confidence → Loss of vulnerability → Loss of true self

The nurturing style a child experiences will determine how she will think about herself and the world at a later stage. If a child's needs are not met by the parents, the child might grow up to have an unhealthy, insecure attachment and over-dependency with the parents, which may lead to Borderline Personality Disorder (BPD). This person will have issues in a romantic relationship where the co-dependency needs to now shift to the partner. This person will consistently seek approval from the parents, and will not be comfortable making decisions for themselves or with the partner. Such a person who hasn't learnt to rely on herself, will not be able to create healthy boundaries and a satisfying romantic relationship with her partner. On the other hand, a safe and reliable nurturing style will let a person enter adulthood with a better sense of self, and let her form relationships with a secure attachment style.

Comparison with others is a big cause of insecurity in our lives. It may be tempting to think of comparison as a valuable tool for self-evaluation, motivation, and growth, but it is of more harm and value. Whereas, every time I applied this concept in my life in the last ten years, I found more harm than value. However while interacting with others and especially my clients, I have seen the ugly side of comparison many a times. Suppose Elon grew up in a household where achievements were valued more than emotions. Elon would constantly compare his own achievements with that of his siblings. This was the source of great tension between him and his siblings, creating envy and jealousy between them. When he grew up, he extended this tendency to compare and his jealousy to everyone around him. He would feel bad about himself when he saw others getting more successful than him. Comparison would quickly give way to competition, and unknowingly he would give himself the impossible target of being the best at everything. This feeling of competition depleted his self-esteem and confidence, and eventually led to depression.

Comparison puts us in a frenzy of insecurity, especially when so much information is available on social media. Without realizing, we end up comparing ourselves with others on the basis of inaccurate information. People usually share edited/filtered realities of their lives which we then take to be true. In this way, we see the perfection in their lives, but the imperfections never comes to the fore. So, when we compare ourselves to such "perfect" people we think that we're the only ones who are in a rut, while the reality is anything but that. As Steve Furtick explains, "The reason we struggle with insecurity is because we compare our behind-the-scenes with everyone else's highlight reel." Any form of comparison with others, be it about looks or success, is only a big distraction in your life. Comparison zaps all motivation from life, and steals our ability to look at those things that really matter to us.

Many a times our insecurities are so deeply ingrained that it becomes difficult for us to see through them. The same was the case with one of my clients. During my sessions with her, we had the following conversation:

Me: What are you struggling with?

Client: It's my office. My colleague may get the promotion that I deserve. I don't like him.

Me: Why don't you like him?

Client: He doesn't like me either. He's very cunning, and knows how to get everyone on his side. I don't even know why he's being selected for the promotion. I don't like his working style. If he gets the promotion, I will quit.

Me: What do you fear will happen if he gets the promotion?

Client: I'm more deserving and committed. I've been with the company for five years. I've put in so much time and effort. I don't want this opportunity to pass me by.

Me: What would happen if your colleague gets the promotion?

Client: It will be so unfair. I will feel very left out and embarrassed. What will my other colleagues think of me?

Me: Have you felt like this before?

Client: Yes.

Me: Can you tell me about your earliest memory where you felt the same way?

Client: I felt like this when I was in the sixth grade. I was running for class president. The girl who was running against me was very popular in class and had a lot of friends. I felt she would easily overshadow me, and so she did.

Me: Now as an adult, when you look back, do you see that situation any differently?

Client: Now it doesn't seem to be such a big deal as it had felt like back then. But at that time I had been too embarrassed to go to school the next day, and I didn't even congratulate my rival after her win.

Me: Would you be comfortable in trying out a role reversal? How would you feel if you were in the shoes of your rival? How would you want others to respond to you?

Client: I would feel very joyous and want everyone to be my friend, even the person who lost.

Me: Do you now see any reason for feeling threatened by your childhood classmate or your colleague?

Client: Not really. I can see it's mostly in my mind.

Me: Have you ever felt condescending towards someone who lost a competition? What were your feeling towards such a person?

Client: I have always had respect for people who had the courage to stand up in front of others and perform in a competition. I wouldn't judge them on whether they won or lost.

Me: What do you think you can do differently in your current situation?

Client: I will carry a healthy spirit, and work on my skills. As long as I give my best, I don't have anything to regret. If I hadn't been so competitive in my life, I would have been more accepting and lighthearted. What a waste it was to be so jealous and fearful for all these years!

Different situations bring up different insecurities and call for tailored course of actions. Some will require you to accept others and yourself. Others will require you to develop certain skills and techniques. Another course of action is to have an honest conversation with others, instead of just assuming things about them. Listed below is a self-guided exercise to help you get in touch with your insecurities.

1. Pick a situation that is not working in your life. Look at what makes you feel insecure about this situation.

____

2. Look deeply and try to understand what makes you feel like this.

____

3. What is the fear that is attached with this?

____

4. How much of this is a fact, and how much are you assuming?

____

5. Now that you see things clearly, can you assess the situation any differently? Write at least four-five things that you would do differently with this new understanding.

____

6. If you can't accept people the way they are, there is

usually something in you that prevents you from doing so. Write down how you can bring a shift in your thoughts to accept yourself and others for who you/they are.

—————————————————————————

7. For the situation under discussion, what are the alternate courses of action available to you? Write down four-five possible choices.

—————————————————————————

8. What are some mental/behavioral roadblocks that may prevent you from taking these actions?

—————————————————————————

9. Roadblocks indicate yet another layer that needs to be peeled off. Start again with (2) with this roadblock in mind.

10. Intentionally try to be vulnerable with people around you. Help other people succeed. Be comfortable in feeling uncomfortable instead of quickly distancing others or over-pleasing them.

When you are doing this, it's important to surround yourself with people who can support you in this transition.

CHAPTER 7

Don't Resent, Be PRESENT

"The secret of health for both mind and body is not to mourn for the past, worry about the future, or anticipate troubles. But to live in the present moment wisely and honestly." - Buddha

It's rather fashionable these days to preach about living in the present. It sounds good, that's true, but what does it really mean? What does it look like? Is it really possible to live in the now, even for just a few moments? Isn't "living in the present" meant only for the yogis and monks? Can you live in the present when you have tens of thousands of tasks to complete? Isn't it for the retired? I had these questions when I came across the mantra of "living in the present". It seemed boring, and a rather heavy topic to explore. I would rather hang out with my friends, go to the gym, or watch TV.

However, during my meditation practice, I discovered that my "default setting" was to live in the past. My past emotional experiences wouldn't leave me even in the present. I'd like to share a personal story here. I was very close to my uncle who was a father figure in my life. I had shared many beautiful moments with him while growing up. His sudden demise left my entire family in shock. We had spoken to him the night before he died. The next morning, when I heard the news of his untimely death it was a shock. He had passed away in his sleep. I was in denial about it for several years. With every ring of the doorbell, I would hope to see him standing outside the door. I felt guilty about getting over his memories, and I felt obligated to relieve them every second. When I went out, I missed him. All my conversations with my family would only be about him. I would think of myself as a bad person if I let myself enjoy the present moment. I wanted to stop anything good from happening in my life. I gave up looking after myself. I stopped meeting people. I wasn't attracted to anyone romantically. And after a couple of years, this became the normal state of my life. While meditating, I realized how I was denying myself the chance to live in the present. And, that was destroying my personality, thought processes, social life, and career. My love life was non-existent. I was a mere shell of myself. Meditation helped me shift my consciousness back into the present moment, and I started to accept my uncle's death. Slowly I started letting go of his haunting memories. It was fascinating to see how my life turned around quickly after that. I lost several pounds; felt lighter and brighter with each passing day. I made new friends and started my own business. I started choosing my present experiences consciously, and life started to flow effortlessly.

If living in the past is dangerous, so is living in the future. We don't just plan for our future, we end up fantasizing about the glory that the future beholds. Both living in the past or the future is escapism from reality. For instance, people who were once rich or famous tend to draw their identity from their past. If someone was popular and successful in school, they stay stuck in the "cool" persona even in adulthood. A retired person can't stop talking about his working days. Someone who is driven by his dreams may not be able to appreciate the beauty of the present. An executive who is putting in long hours to get a promotion might be unable to appreciate a simple dinner with his wife or a hug from his kids. So you can see that a person who is too fearful about the future will not be able to enjoy the present.

We rely on our past to make sense of our present. However past memories can be largely fabricated. Research has shown that our memories are rewritten every time the brain remembers them. The way we see our past is constantly evolving. The brain recreates details about your memories as per your current situation. The brain keeps you trapped in your past, and keeps you away from your present. Say, John often attributes his lack of success to a past event which happened twenty years ago, and fails to see resources and opportunities in front of him today. Judy separated from her husband five years ago after many years of an abusive marriage, and she still mistrusts men. She does this to avoid the pain and hurt she felt in the past. We often use the past as a crutch to hide our incapability. When we dwell on our past, we stop learning from it. As a result, we don't develop the skills required to deal with current situations effectively. If John acquires new skills to stay secure in his job, then his past is already healed. Similarly, if Judy realizes that all men are not the same, and learns to put up boundaries and focus on self-care in relationships, she would be less fearful of entering another relationship. One can't go back in the past to change it. The change can only be made in the now, and this change automatically heals the past. There are times when we're stuck in our past due to a lack of closure, such as a sudden loss of a loved one, being laid off from your job without notice, or being cheated in a relationship. Not always will you get the closure to help you understand what went wrong. In such circumstances, it is important to accept the fact that you can't do anything about what has happened, and that in itself has to be the closure.

Everyone is looking for happiness and is busy in the pursuit of it. We feel that happiness will come to us when the weekend arrives, when we go for a much-awaited vacation to the Bahamas, when we retire early, or when we win the lottery. We think we need to wait for these events to enjoy living in the moment. But what do we do when these events occur? We want to party and make merry by drinking alcohol, over-indulging in food and sleep. Then on a Sunday we worry about Monday. During vacations, we can't stop ourselves from glancing at our phones and checking for emails from office. When we eventually retire, we yearn for the young life again. Basically, we can either choose to be in the present or not; there are no two ways about it. Have you ever sat down and asked yourself, "Why don't I live in the present? What stops me from being in the now? What is it that I'm running away from?"

Traumatic experiences from the past make us worry about the future. But just like we have no control over the past, similarly we have no control over the future. I'm not saying that you shouldn't think about your past or your future, all I'm warning you against is overthinking about it. Over-thinkers are prisoners to their own minds. No matter how much we would like to control our future, it's never going to happen the way we want it to. When we worry about the unpredictability of our future, we constantly live in insecurity, self-doubt, and become victims of potential trauma in the future. We may live in the future due to our learned behavior from our families and friends. If someone we look up to has the tendency to over think about the future, we tend to follow similar patterns. We are also being socially conditioned from our childhood to live in the future. We have been constantly warned by our parents and teachers to "think about our future". When we operate like this for many years, we become habituated with living in the future. Comparison is yet another reason for overthinking. It makes us analyze our past critically in the present moment. Suppose Tang gets up early every morning to sip hot tea while looking out of the window to see the woods and the sunrise. But instead of enjoying the view, he constantly worries about how he needs to acquire a Ferrari since his best friend just got one. He even gets irritated when his wife asks him to accompany her on a morning walk.

Comparison gives us unrealistic expectations about our lives and creates self-doubt. This makes us fear the perceived lack in the future. Denial of your present situation is also one cause that can keep you stuck in the future. Someone who has a bad relationship with his/her spouse is trying to avoid working on themselves and their relationship by thinking that everything will get sorted on its own. One of my friends confided in me about her relationship woes. She was fretting about the future. It seemed to her that her relationship will eventually end in separation. I asked her what she was doing in the present to make her relationship work. She looked at me with big blank eyes, which conveyed clearly that all she was doing at present was worry about the separation. Even though it is obvious that we need to take actions in the now to make things better, but our past baggage and our worries about the future keep us so engrossed that we fail to take actions in time. We forget that we have the power to create the life we desire by taking the necessary actions in the now. Until we shift our actions and behaviors to the "present" nothing will shift. Some small positive steps that you can take now are having a heartfelt conversation that you have been putting off for many years, speaking with your partner in a softer tone, working on the skills that you need to develop, throwing away the cigarette or the drink, closing your eyes and meditating. Action begins in the NOW!

When we let our mind wander on its own, we let it pick up whatever memory it wants. It jumps from one memory to the other and creates an unending web. Have you caught yourself reliving embarrassing moments from your past, or over glorifying your past or your future? Have you experienced trouble sleeping because you couldn't disconnect from your thoughts? Have you ruminated on events or on actions of people to find a hidden meaning in them? Have you been brought out of your reveries by someone shaking you? How many times have you been immersed in thinking about things that are not in your control? All these are signs of you being an over thinker. Over thinkers believe that their "thoughts" can generate a solution, however nothing can be further from the truth. Rather they lose peace of mind, get filled with self-doubt, become indecisive, suffer from lack of sleep, anxiety, hypertension, and chronic stress, will become numb or agitated, swing from one extreme to the other, etc. If we don't live in the now, we can't meet our emotional and physical needs, and neither that of our loved ones. The anxiety of the future or remorse for the past will never let us be in touch with our current resources.

When I started to meditate, I began to realize that I could consciously choose to live in the present. We have all heard the phrase "let go of the negative thoughts". To do that I started to fixate on positive thoughts. This again took me to the future where I wanted to purposefully see what my future would look like. I was imagining all my desires and fantasies coming true in the future. But this too is unnecessary excitation for the mind. Whether the thoughts are negative or positive, too much of them are harmful, if we're not in the now. Most likely there is a deep-seated cause that keeps us glued to the past or the future. It could be insecurity, fear, embarrassing moments, or may be the need to recreate a pleasant version of a past memory. The past is past. Whether they were good or bad experiences, it doesn't matter because they only exist in the metaphysical realm of our memories now. However we keep reliving these experiences in the current moment as if they are happening to us now. Relationships remain sour even years after a negative confrontation. One embarrassing moment can leave us in anxiety forever, as if it is constantly repeating itself in our lives.

Meditation is a powerful technique that can help you to get back to the present moment. It has the power to raise the curtains and let you see through your fears and your hopes. A few meditation techniques are described below which you can practice daily. Start with ten-fifteen minutes of meditation daily. You can even break it into smaller sessions of five minutes each throughout the day.

Chanting: Repeat a word in your mind that is sacred to you (I use "om") and keep a rosary in your hand. Repeat the word silently or utter it softly. This will get you back to the now. If your mind begins to wander, get back to the rosary to stay in the now.

Walking meditation: This can be practiced whenever you're walking. With every step you take, be aware of how your feet are touching the ground and how you're breathing. Bring all your senses of sight, sound, smell, and touch into the now with every step you take. Experience the stimuli that your senses are receiving. You can use this technique in other activities too such as eating, sitting, and speaking.

Breathing meditation: Focus on the sensation of air flowing through your nostrils as you breathe in and out. As you breathe in, become aware of the thoughts in your mind. As you breathe out, let your thoughts flow out of your mind. The goal is not to push out any thoughts, but to just let them flow without holding on to them. This is a very powerful mediation which helps to resolve mental and bodily problems. You can choose to do this meditation with your eyes closed or open. Everyone has their own preference. If you wish to meditate with your eyes open, you can keep a candle lit in front of you so that you can focus on the flame to keep your thoughts from wandering.

Nidra meditation: You can do this meditation at night before sleeping or even during your lunch break. You can sit straight on a comfortable chair and relax your body, or lie down straight. Let your arms and legs be slightly spread out. Take a couple of deep breaths when you start this meditation. This is a quick and easy way to get rid of thoughts and focus on the meditation. In this meditation, you will slowly move your focus on different body parts, from your head to your toes. When you breathe in, focus on a specific body part. While you're breathing out, feel all the tension flowing out of your body. Focus longer on the body part where you're experiencing any discomfort. If you do this meditation at night, it will help you fall asleep easily. You will experience a more refreshing sleep.

There are lots of other meditational practices which help you stay in the now. These exercises give us a break from the mechanical life we lead and make us aware of how we react when a stimuli gets presented. It shows us how much we're gripped by our thoughts, and how we react without thinking. Another exercise is the **love and compassion meditation**. Loving others, as you would love yourself and your dear ones, helps you cultivate compassion for yourself and for others. After the breathing meditation, close your eyes for a minute and visualize yourself sitting in an open space. Feel the unconditional love and compassion for yourself that you have been craving from others. After you feel content, visualize your friends and family around you, and extend the same feeling of love and compassion to them. Keep on adding more and more people in your thoughts to whom you want to extend unconditional love and compassion. Family → Friends → Relatives → Colleagues → Neigbours → State → Country → World.

We humans move along the axis of time in a unidirectional manner. This means, in human experience, the fleeting moment that is passing us by is really "the now". A second has passed since when you started reading this paragraph, but it is already your past, which can never be relived, albeit only in your memories. Life is in the here, now, and is passing by right now, right here, now, here, new moment, gone. Without connecting to your thoughts as they are occurring in the now, or experiencing the stimuli as you're receiving them from your senses, aren't we disconnected from the now, our real reality? Then what's the point of sacrificing it by constantly reliving the memories of the past or by dreaming about a future? It's just a bad habit that can be broken. And, meditation is the powerful tool that can let us achieve this goal by helping us let go of unwanted thoughts and reactions. It helps us curate our thoughts and habits which let us experience the now while staying in harmony with our mind, body, and soul.

When you start doing these mediations, you will see that you're getting rid of discriminatory thoughts, judgmental biases, and the blaming attitude. This leaves you with a calm and balanced state of mind which allows you to be in the now. You will experience better concentration, physical improvements, alleviation of high blood pressure, anxiety, hyper vigilance (PTSD), hyperactive behavior (ADHD), eating disorders, addictions, and more.

It's not very hard to live in the moment and to be mindful even though it may seem so when you're about to begin the journey. Remaining peaceful and being observant helps us acknowledge what we're really feeling. It helps us to know which emotions are stemming from the past and which are from the future. Being in the moment helps us make the right decisions. Instead of getting overwhelmed by our thoughts, we learn how to question them. It helps in developing new patterns of behavior and actions by freeing us from distractions and reactions. Once we understand how our own mind works, it becomes easier to understand others. We feel less threatened and develop oneness with others, and refuse to take part in their dramas. It is natural for the human mind to stumble and trip on events that happens in life, but meditating on a regular basis help us maintain the balance needed to lead our lives effectively.

"Those running behind happiness have never found it. Happiness is a mirage."

CHAPTER 8

ANGER is D-anger!

"**H**olding on to anger is like grasping a hot coal with the intent of throwing it at someone else. You're the one who gets burned." – Buddha

Anger is a natural and universal emotion that occurs when we perceive being cornered by someone, or if a big resource is at stake. In the modern world, this can manifest in many ways. Office politics often makes you feel cornered when a big resource, such as a promotion, might be at stake. A driver makes a dangerous maneuver, making you feel angry about their lack of skill or poor judgment. When you learn that you are being gossiped about, you feel angry as your reputation is at stake. When your neighbor has a late night party and is disturbing you with loud music, you feel angry because they are intruding upon your privacy. We feel anger on our politicians for acting irresponsibly with our national resources. We all experience the pangs of anger from time to time, but do we even understand them, or know how to deal with them effectively?

I'd like to narrate my own experience here. I married my husband and moved to a new country, which was a big transition for me. Marriage, getting used to living with someone, and dealing with the culture difference in a new country, starting my career from scratch again, having no friends or family of my own, everything was overwhelming. However it was not as big a challenge as adjustment to each other's style of anger. Without me consciously realizing I was irritated and frustrated at the changes I was going through. not knowing how to deal with my emotions, I was anxious and sad. This was building up in me and I started

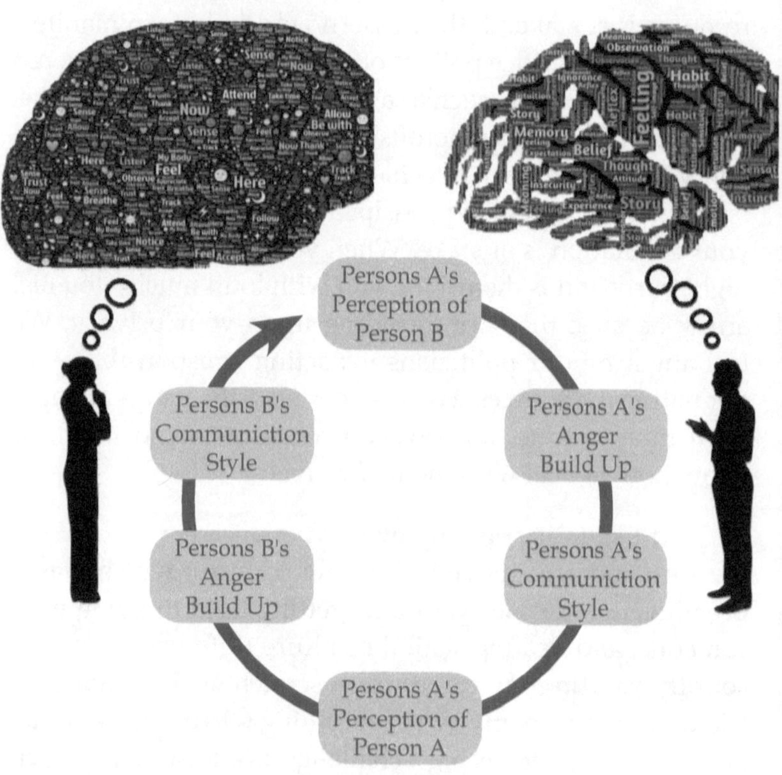
Persons A's Perception of Person B
Persons A's Anger Build Up
Persons A's Communiction Style
Persons A's Perception of Person A
Persons B's Anger Build Up
Persons B's Communiction Style

to slowly withdrawing into my shell. My husband, took my challenge as personal attack and he would get angry at me in return. His style of anger was more direct, destructive, and open, whereas mine was sulking, freezing, and remaining silent. Without us realizing, this slowly spiraled into ugly fights, screaming matches, punching the walls, not talking for days, and ultimately a fractured relationship. Without us knowing how to deal with our respective angers, we caused immense mental harm to each other and our relationship.

Both the people in this diagram are observing each other's behavior, actions, and words in their own ways. Their perception of the other person is triggering a response in their own minds. The feelings of irritation and frustration towards the other person will build up as anger, which gets expressed through their communication styles. This causes an equal and opposite reaction, and the situation gets out of control. No one is taking responsibility for their own perceptions, and instead throwing the blame outside. This chain reaction can only end in an explosion.

Anger is often mistaken as a feeling that arises in us as a result of an external situation. Anger is like an iceberg. Its visible manifestation triggered by an external source is just the tip. The deeper portion of anger is internal and invisible. Anger often has roots in the meanings we attach to an event or situation, which are in turn driven by our beliefs and values inherited from our families and culture, or are shaped by past experiences. If we grew up in an environment where the caregivers openly exhibited their anger, we imbibe the same expression of anger in us. In certain cultures, anger is seen as a right reserved for the elders, and the young ones are obligated to be the victims of their fury and not react. At the same time, movies, video games, and popular culture propagate the use of unhealthy anger towards others. Societal norms of how one must behave according to gender don't allow us to express our true emotions. "Big boys don't cry, and girls don't yell". These beliefs lead men to openly display their anger without feeling any guilt. At the same time, girls feel guilty about expressing their anger. Say Christian and Christy were siblings who grew up in a family where it was okay for boys to yell, but not so for girls. Christian became a bully by the time he was a teenager. He learnt to express all his negative emotions through anger. Whereas, Christy was never allowed to express her anger. Her emotions were never allowed to have a voice, and she learned to suppress them. Gradually she lost touch with the anger inside her and submitted to the desires of her family. By the time she was a teenager, her suppressed anger made her emotionally distant from her family. She became an introvert, and targeted this anger inwards. She became a chain-smoker and over-eater.

Let's see how anger makes us dance on its tunes. We all express anger differently in different situations. Anger can manifest verbally or non-verbally in three different ways: passive, aggressive, and assertive. **Passive anger** is the veiled expression of anger. Instead of openly stating his dissatisfaction, this person will make veiled comments and beat about the bush to make others submit to his thoughts. To the recipient of such form of anger, this feels like betrayal and backstabbing. The anger manifests as silent treatment, sulking, blaming, excuses, obstructionism, playing the victim card, sarcasm, backhanded compliments, rolling of the eyes, and other non-verbal cues. Say a teenager lashes out at his mother saying, "I'm grown up now. Stop treating me like a child. I can't take it anymore." The mother who felt offended by her child's yelling retorted back, "Well, do what you want to," and walks away. Instead of having a clear communication, she resorts to passive anger by giving him the silent treatment, passing sarcastic statements, and rolling her eyes. She knows that by doing this she will be able to control her son's behavior by inciting shame in him.

Aggressive anger is an outward visible display of anger, which shows up as verbal or physical rage. This often takes the form of bullying, blackmailing, accusing, shouting, bickering, throwing or breaking things, harming yourself or others. The purpose of this behavior is to subdue and humiliate the other person into submission. Often the person displaying this type of anger is trying to hide his guilt, shame, and responsibility. If your partner doesn't comply with the rules of your family, you may feel ashamed and lash out at your partner. Aggressive anger is the most toxic and abusive form of anger. It destroys relationships and the mental health of everyone involved. The best recourse available to the recipient of this type of anger is to remove themselves from the presence of the angry person. Both the types of anger, passive and aggressive, are essentially egoistical and leave no room for open discussions and resolution of the underlying issues. People who display any of these forms of anger often lash out unreasonably at the people who are not expected to retaliate. Even if they do so, the effects are generally not threatening. For example, a man whose boss yelled at him goes home and picks up a fight with this wife and scolds his children. However, he still keeps a good rapport with the people in his office and with his social circle.

Assertive anger, on the other hand, is the most productive way of dealing with underlying issues. In assertive anger, you own up to your feelings and take responsibility for it without associating your feelings with someone else's actions. You realize that your emotions come from your own problems. Also, you don't take other's actions personally. In this state, you're able to express yourself in terms of your own feelings. You don't act out trying to blame, control, and dominate others, or force them to see your point of views. When you're assertive you're flexible, empathetic, non-threatening, and act with the intent of clearing the air with no hidden agenda. In this state, you're open to other's feelings and don't pass judgments on the basis of "should", "must", or "is". You respect other's boundaries and space as much as you respect your own. Anger is like a friend to an assertive person; it acts like an intense emotion which gets you in touch with your core beliefs. Channeling your anger appropriately can help you connect with others through compassion, understanding, and love.

If the wife wants to buy a dress which the husband thinks is out of their budget, he can have one of the following responses:

Passive: Walks away unenthusiastically with an eye roll.

Aggressive: Yells, "Why don't you understand that we have a budget to meet? I shouldn't have to remind you again and again."

Assertive: Empathically expresses, "I like your taste in clothes. This is such a pretty dress. But I'm afraid that there's a financial constraint. How do you propose we fit this into our budget?"

Anger, as a physiological response, is very powerful when we know how to control it. On the other hand, uncontrolled anger can be highly destructive for relationships and health. At its heart, directing anger at yourself (substance abuse, self-harm, over-eating, starvation) or others (situations, family members, friends, and strangers) is blame. And, blaming stops you from looking at the root of the issue. According to research, sustained anger can result in heart disease, high blood pressure, anxiety, insomnia, and a weak immune system. Anger alienates us from our loved ones as it is often them at whom we lash out the most. It creates a feeling of fear and distrust, especially when the relationship is not equal. Take for instance, a parent yelling at his child. It may result in the child getting fearful and not wanting to open up to the parent. Such a child learns to repress her emotions, and will be fearful about developing open relationships in the future. Anger can cause distance and resentment in a relationship, especially when the anger is bottled up and not expressed healthily. We may avoid discussing our feelings with our partners in the fear of having an argument, but this may cause us to feel resentment towards our partners over time. If we end up venting out at a third person, it will form an unhealthy triangle. This will stop us from working out the relationship issues with our partners.

Anger causes tension and frustration in relationships and makes us jump to conclusions quickly about the other person. These negative feelings arise when we're trying to change the other person using anger as a weapon. The key is to remember that we never have control over the thoughts and actions of another person. Trying to push our agenda on to somebody else will only result in hostility. Hostility manifests itself not only through violence, attack, revenge, but also through sarcasm, teasing, and passive obstructiveness. At this point, all communication shuts down, and we solicit an equal reaction from the other person, who now views us as an adversary.

Blaming, criticizing, yelling, and passive aggressive behavior make us feel powerful at the moment. But do we ask ourselves the question, "What have I gained in the long run?" At the end of the day, the other person has lost his vulnerability towards us, and is now defensive, ready to hit back or withdraw. A once intimate and precious relationship is lost. Emotions can never be validated. No one's hurt is bigger than the other's. If you have anger issues in your life, you may want to consider seeing a therapist, counsellor, or taking some online courses.

We have heard that it's the small things that matter in life, and this is true even in relationships. When we feel that our small needs are not being met by the other person, we let the bigger things slip away as well. Taking care of the small needs in a relationship helps us bond with each other through empathy and compassion. It makes us feel loved and understood. It could be remembering the special occasions in our partner's life, their likes or dislikes, appreciating them for who they are, or helping them in their everyday chores. On the other hand, when we forget our small promises, the other person feels unloved and unimportant. Take for instance, a situation where you requested your spouse to help you in a task that is important to you. But you had to remind her every day about it. Or, your partner doesn't make efforts on date nights, and is disinterested. You requested your family to be nice to the person you were dating, but they bring out their knives when they met your partner. In all of these examples, the person whom you had trusted didn't follow through on their commitments. If small needs are not met in a relationship, it leads to irritation, frustration, and resentment. And, in a relationship which has resentment, we enter a battle to prove the validity of our emotions which have been hurt, in order to win empathy from the other person. In this stalemate, we don't offer any empathy or compassion, and we don't shift our behavior as that would show that we accepted our mistake and took the blame. When people lose empathy and compassion in a relationship, it leads to criticism, defensiveness, arguments, and eventually stonewalling. This pattern, if sustained, eventually morphs into revenge. Once this happens, the relationship becomes a series of come-backs, a battle of one-upmanship. What if my friends embarrass me in public with their jibes, and I become the butt of jokes in a party? More likely than not my natural instinct will be to mark that moment in my mind and redeem myself in the future. I will be looking for similar situations where I can return the favor. Even if a hint of resentment comes into a relationship, it becomes a cycle of proving your dominance over the other, things eventually ending on a bitter note. This is not only limited between friends or partners, but can be seen in any relationship – siblings, teacher-student, anything. But this is mostly seen between couples where insensitive behavior towards each other is easily justified. Both the people in the relationship think they are justified in their actions, however insensitive, callous, and downright malicious those actions might be.

Anger can be managed if we work on –

- Self-esteem

- Competitive spirit

- Striving for perfection

- Embracing your mistakes

- Expressing your feeling

- Practicing gratitude

- Positive language

- Engaging in creative activities

- Physical exercise

I described at the beginning of this chapter how my relationship with my husband spiraled into anger. This caused us tremendous hurt and anguish. I ultimately decided that something needed to be done about it. I was ready to take the first step, even if it meant a one sided effort. The first thing I did was to own up to my anger. No one has the power to make me angry. I realized that the source of my anger was the sudden shift in my life. I was in a new country living with a person with different customs and beliefs than that of mine. It felt that my entire existence was being shifted and I felt very anxious. My natural reaction was to go and speak about this to my husband. And I was expecting him to understand, be compassionate and help solve my issues. I forgot that he had his own baggage and expectations too. I realized how our expectations of each other resulted in resentment and distrust in the relationship. I also realized that not all the things my husband was doing were to hurt me. When he was angry, he was displaying his frustrations and irritations. But the delivery of the message was embedded with a lot of anger and harsh words, and the message was getting lost. If we were to get out of this rut, we had to learn to see beyond the antics. Instead of focusing my attention should on how I was being spoken on, or to my bruised ego, I focused on my needs. I made a mental note of my needs which were not being met in the relationship and were causing me hurt. I spoke to my husband about my feeling in terms of how I felt about them. By doing so, I was taking responsibility of my emotions and didn't pinning the blame on him or others externally (instead of saying "You make me angry," or "You will never understand," or "You care only about your TV and not me," I would say, "I feel angry and sad when I don't have your full attention," or "I feel left out when I'm not understood," or "I need to connect with you emotionally instead of watching TV.") This enabled us to have a discussion in which we could listen to each other's concerns with empathy and compassion. This helped us lower our defenses and we could extend an olive branch whenever things got heated. We were no longer making personal attacks. This was the biggest breakthrough in our relationship. With every successive discussion, we were making real progress instead of having screaming matches. When our discussion would get heated and anger would creep back in, we would call a time out. Distancing for twenty minutes really helped to calm down the fight-flight response. During the twenty minutes, I would make it a point to think of my anger in terms of my emotions. This helped me pick up the discussion back again with a gentle tap on his shoulder.

The following is an exercise that can help you get in touch with your anger and take responsibility for it.

1. Sit by yourself in a comfortable spot and take deep breaths to free your mind from any gripping thoughts.

2. Think about a situation in which you felt really angry on someone.

____

____

3. Recall how you reacted and expressed your anger.

____

____

4. Know your anger style. How do you display anger (passive, aggressive, assertive)?

____

5. Look deep within yourself and see what really triggered you.

____

____

6. When we express our anger at someone, we believe that they deserve it as they did something bad to us. And, we know that we have the right to express our anger on them and get away. But it's time to let go of control. It's time to let go of perfectionism. Write down how much, and in what way you are ready to loosen up in this particular situation.

____

____

7. I know and understand how other's actions may

have a negative impact on you. You may feel compelled to protect yourself by throwing a fit. But you don't have the right to abuse anyone by bursting out in anger.

8. Own up to your triggers, emotions, and reactions.

Own up to your anger → Work on your fear, stress, anxiety, and temperament → Let go of control (situation or person) → Express your feelings in terms of yourself → Listen actively to the other party → Be compassionate → Apologize for your behavior → Forgive yourself and others → Demonstrate compassion and conciliatory behavior from the next time onwards

9. Most behavioral shifts must be practiced before they become permanent. It's important to take time out and rehearse in your mind how you can take control over your emotions. When you feel very angry in a situation, you can –

- Take a break from the situation for twenty minutes. It's important not to speak when you're stewing from inside as your words and actions may be coming from a place of spite in some moments.

- In these twenty minutes, you can expend your energy by going for a run, dancing, tearing paper, punching a bag, or screaming into a pillow. You can also practice breathing meditations, take a relaxing bath, stroll in the nature. Do anything that can help your mind and muscles relax.

- After twenty minutes, ask yourself the question,

"What triggered me?" Think in terms of your own actions and feelings.

- Once you're in touch with your own feelings, you can resume the conversation by being responsible, and by speaking in terms of your own feelings (this expresses vulnerability), with empathy and compassion. Remember, confronting someone may be tempting, but it will ultimately add fuel to the fire.

- Remember that the other party also has their own feelings and challenges to present to you. The other person may still be fuming, and may not know how to control their anger. You still need to remain cool and calm, and practice assertive expression of anger. It takes one to break the chain.

Remember words, gestures, and actions triggered by anger are destructive, and create a bad memory in everyone's mind. This later becomes a baggage which starts showing up in every subsequent conversation now and then. This will cause anger to build up, and if not mindfully watched and corrected, it will lead to distancing, barriers, defenses, hidden agendas, violence, and domestic problems. We will lose love and support which is important for our survival. Remember the person is more important than the argument.

CHAPTER 9

Bomb the Wall of Shame!

"**Shame is internalized when one is abandoned. Abandonment is the precise term to describe how one loses one's authentic self and ceases to exist psychologically.**" — John Bradshaw

Shame is a powerful emotion that makes one feel defective, unacceptable, and damaged beyond repair. It is the feeling that makes one feel less of a human being, incapable and unworthy. It is a psychological prison which binds us to the people in our lives in an unhealthy manner. Or, prevents us from breaking the shackles and achieving something on our own. However not all shame is bad. Healthy shame drives you to apologize and make amends when you break an interpersonal bridge by hurting someone's feelings, or violating someone's dignity. Healthy shame makes us human, keeps us in our limits. On the other hand, toxic shame is not natural but acquired. It is debilitating and makes you feel unworthy, leaving you susceptible to abuse. You see yourself as a bad person for feeling a certain way, and think that you have no place in this world. Toxic shame makes you withdraw, preventing you from opening up, or overcompensating to hide something in you. Toxic shame is what makes a child hide behind the parents when guests visit. Toxic shame is what makes an adult please those who make them feel inadequate. It is a feeling of vulnerability that overwhelms us.

Shame and guilt are highly correlated, but they are not the same. I couldn't say it better than Brené Brown: "*Shame is a focus on self, guilt is a focus on behavior. Shame is, 'I'm bad.' Guilt is, 'I did something bad.' Guilt: 'I'm sorry. I made a mistake.' Shame: 'I'm sorry. I'm a mistake.'"*

The same event or situation in our lives can be seen from various angles. Relationships are particularly multi-dimensional and are affected by various facets of our personalities and beliefs. In the chapters on Judgement and Anger I described how I dealt with these aspects in my marital life. I also discovered a different level of shame inside me after my marriage. In my husband's family, it was normal to share every tiny detail with each other. This was something new to me, and I hadn't seen this in my own family. I wasn't comfortable with this level of intimacy, and I was a bit reserved with them. My in-laws started resenting me for this. I could see disappointment in their eye rolls and facial expressions. They kept suggesting how I should be more talkative, or how we won't be a family until we share everything with each other. Their disappointment in me aroused my shame. I started to overcompensate by pleasing them and going out of my comfort zone to share minute details with them. However, nothing I did seemed to be enough. I continued seeing disappointment in their eyes. My shame kept spiraling inside me, and I kept trying harder and harder to please them. And, in this whole process, I felt judged and insulted, as if I had failed to live up to their expectations. Who I was didn't matter anymore, what became important was the fact if I could perform.

Shame is instilled in us through different avenues – family, religion, culture, society, gender-based expectations, school, media, etc. Shame distorts our personality. People who live in shame are prone to suppressing their emotions, often avoid relationships and engaging with the community. Shame is often accompanied by other mental states, and by emotions of envy, anger, rage, and anxiety. This makes shame a powerful and dangerous emotion.

More often than not shame is rooted in childhood experiences.

- A child, in early life, draws a sense of security by the empathetic mirroring of emotions he receives from his caregivers. The caregivers are the people with whom he develops his first bonds. The parents mirror their child by matching their tone and gestures. This validates the child of her self-worth. However, when the caregivers are too engrossed with their own lives, the implicit trust and security in the child is broken. The child now gets the message that she is not important, that her feelings are insignificant, and that her needs are secondary to those of her parents'. This induces a feeling of shame in the child. The child feels abandoned as her need for security is not met.

- When the parents openly fight amongst themselves, and overexpose their child to their animosity, the child feels emotionally torn, and is numbed and depressed. Take for instance, a situation where Jon's parents constantly fight in the open. After the fight, his mother usually comes to his room and cries. She expresses her misery, and moans about how she's suffering in this marriage only because of him. His mother leans onto him for comfort, and Jon feels obligated to support his mother. This is in clear violation of a healthy boundary between a parent and a child. Jon has now become a "lost child". He has lost his childhood. Instead of drawing security from his parents, now he is the provider of security to his mother. This is too heavy a burden on his little shoulders, too big a shoe to walk in. Jon is a "surrogate spouse" to his mother. The mother enjoys this sense of security she drives from her son, and doesn't feel the need to improve her relationship with her husband. This will have devastating consequences for Jon. He will be reluctant to explore himself or his needs as his primary focus will be to fulfill those of his mother's. Such children grow up to be adults who are too ashamed to explore their sexuality and have romantic relationships. Even if they do get married, they will feel shame in bonding with their spouses and kids until all of them agree to satisfy his mother.

- Sometimes parents may express their disappointment verbally or non-verbally when their child fails to meet their expectations. This tells the child that she is unworthy, and needs to comply with her caregivers in order to be appreciated. Such a child will suppress herself by spending the rest of her life by pleasing others and seeking their approval. She will not have the courage to do anything on her own, and will be unable to challenge the popular opinion.

- A child may be reprimanded when she is exploring her own needs and drives. This makes the child feel shame in having those needs met. For example, suppose, a toddler who is curious about her surroundings is playing in the lawn with worms and mud. The father scolds and humiliates the child on seeing this, "You're so filthy. Look at what you've done," or "You're such an idiot," etc. Such a child will grow up to have severe issues in expressing herself as an adult.

- When the parents scold the child around other people, it makes the child feel humiliated. The child may now start feeling socially unacceptable.

- The parents may dump their negative emotions of fears, loneliness, and financial insecurity on to their children indirectly. For example, parents may lash out at their kids in frustration because of their own issues. Such children become the scapegoats for the family. Over a prolonged period of time, the children live in toxic shame, believing that anything that goes wrong is because of them. They learn to walk on egg shells to keep their parents happy.

The child reflects the parents, and tries to balance the family to restore and preserve harmony. These children, when they grow up unhealed, look out for partners who can fill the emptiness in them, and take care of their childhood needs. Sigmund Freud mentioned that shame generates defenses of denial, idealization of parents, repression and dissociation of emotions. When parents are shame-based and needy themselves, they turn over to their own children for their narcissistic gratifications; and keep the children at their disposal for their pleasure.

Children who please the parents → Not allowed to know themselves, family rules are imposed (adults are the masters of the child, parents have to be shielded at all times, children are never allowed to think/interpret/choose on their own) → Don't grow with trial and error → Cannot separate from their parents -> Superficial relationship with parents without questioning → Idealization and fantasy-bonding with the parents (parents are next to God) → Similar relationship style in other relationships

People with toxic shame have a disassociation of their private self and external self.

Families with shame-based behavioral patterns usually have role/gender dependent expectations of "should", "must", and "have". Anything beyond this role will not be accepted. In such kinds of dysfunctional families, the system is frozen, static, and unchangeable with rigid cover-ups of the true self.

If the father in the family is not earning well, he may feel shame as he is not able to fulfill his rigid role of being the provider. His shame doesn't let him see the situation clearly and make amends. His private and external selves are disassociated. Instead, he finds the cover-up by blaming other people or situations around him. He pins all hopes on his son who is expected to make up for his failures when he grows up.

Now if his son is successful, the father draws pride

from the son's achievement, and claims it as his own. He praises his son for what he has achieved rather than for who he is as a person. This teaches the son that his identity is driven from his achievements rather than from his personal traits. The son now will be in a mad rush to always be successful. In this way, he will become highly competitive and jealous of others. Thus, the tradition of disassociation of the private and external selves continues in the family.

However, if the son fails to meet the stringent standards imposed on him, he feels empty and unworthy, and shame takes over. The son wants to fix it quickly by any means so that he can get back his father's love and attention. He will become a people-pleaser or a shy person who will never state his needs, since his lack of success makes him feel unworthy.

The son has been denied the experience of connecting to his own feelings, and is highly dependent on his narcissistic father for telling him how to feel and navigate the world. The son may be living in the fantasy that he has a loving relationship with his father, but in reality, their identities have been fused into each other's. Shame tamed the son to believe that "parents are God", and what they decide for you is the best course of action.

In the above example, both father and son never knew what to do beyond their expected roles. They didn't know how to handle their mistakes which in turn created shame in them. A legacy of toxic shame was created. The devastating aspect of toxic shame is multigenerational as people in the family live in denial, rage, hate, depression, repression, idealization, and blame-game. We can't heal what we can't feel.

Controlling others with shame and power as the cover-up for shame

Shame is "a painful feeling of humiliation or distress caused by the consciousness of wrong or foolish behavior" (oxforddictionaries.com). Shame can be a very debilitating emotion, and we all know its power subconsciously. That is why we use it as a weapon to control others. I'd like to share a funny, yet pertinent, example from my life. When I was eight, our family was visiting my uncle's place in another city. I was very fond of eating sweets as a child. One afternoon when no one was around, I saw a cake in the kitchen. Slice by slice, I started devouring the cake. I didn't realize when I had eaten all of it, until just a single piece remained. I hid the remaining cake in the fridge, and pretended as if nothing had happened. At teatime, when my aunt took out the cake from the fridge, I remember her horror at seeing the small piece left. My mother saw the embarrassment on my face and realized what I had done. She shamed me with her glares in front of everyone. Even to this day, I feel uncomfortable when I am the first one to eat. I wait for everyone to help themselves before I can keep food on my plate. In fact, I feel angry at others who eat by themselves without waiting for others. Subconsciously, my mother knew how to control me with shame.

When we harbor the feeling of shame about our past,

we become overly defensive when even a little bit of shame is stirred. Exerting power through anger is the perfect way to misdirect your attention away from the painful feelings hidden inside you, much like how a magician uses misdirection to execute a card trick.

We can use shame to trick ourselves when we feel rejected by others. We don't have any control over how others feel. We can't make them love us. We become addicted to shame because it protects us from the truth that we really have no control over others. However, shame makes us feel as if there is something wrong in us which is why someone doesn't like us. This gives us a false sense of control over the situation. We trick ourselves into believing that if we can change this or that about me, they will like us.

There are certain common traits in a shame-based family. Do you relate to any of these?

- **Control and chaos:** No one is taking responsibility for their lives. Instead of working on improving themselves, they exert power by controlling others in the family. This includes shaming others. This pattern of control is like a chain where each member is trying to exert power based on hierarchy. The control leads to chaos where everyone is striving for power. The father yells at the mother -> The mother yells at the kids -> The eldest sibling yells at the younger one -> The youngest child kicks the dog.

- **Perfectionism:** The expectation of perfection is amplified in the family. A mistake is shamed, hence everyone is carrying out the impossible task of becoming perfect.

- **Blame:** If failure is shamed in the family, the family members will be blaming and criticizing each other. They will be reluctant to admit responsibility.

- **Disassociation and denial:** When we're confronted with shame, we deny our wrong doings or feelings..

- **No talking and no listening:** Discussions in the family will be superficial. Anything which can give rise to shame will be shoved under the carpet.

- **Role-dependent:** When families are role-dependent, there are often rigid tracks of behavior that one must display. Not walking on these rigid tracks will incite shame. For example, a father should be a provider, a mother should a good cook, a daughter must be gentle, a son should be rough and tough, etc.

Identification with the offender

Why would people who were once abused, beaten, abandoned, and toxically shamed, want to play their abuser's role? The answer lies in the dynamic of identification. Offender identification was aptly described by Bettelheim with the phrase "identification with the aggressor". When children, who are shamed and physically hurt, go through psychological pain, they want to get out of it as quickly as possible, as it's too complicated for them to work through their feelings. They cease to identify with themselves, and rather identify with the shaming oppressor; they believe that the oppressor is correct in shaming them. To avoid feeling shameful again, they act out like their oppressors. This is a survival strategy where one feels that they have a better chance of survival if they submit to their aggressors. A classic example of "identification with the aggressor" is the Stockholm Syndrome where a kidnapping victim establishes an emotional bond with the kidnapper. It's used to describe victims who have favorable feelings and behavior towards their abuser, and negative attitudes towards things that go against their abuser's mentality and actions. Therefore, shame-based parents re-enact the trauma for their kids that they had experienced themselves when they were little. They have not learnt to externalize this shame by saying, "Shame on my father for making me feel like this," or "Shame on my mother for doing that to me in public."

Healing the shame

Healing my shame was one of the most rejuvenating experiences of my life. Healing my shame broke down the feeling of inadequacy that I had carried in me all my life, which I had received from my parents, teachers, friends, bosses, colleagues, and the society at large.

Here I want to describe some insights that I have gained from my healing process. I was feeling ashamed during my skirmishes with my in-laws, not because of them but because of my own insecurities, and I would express my discomfort to my husband. However, I didn't know about the shame that my husband had also been carrying inside him because of his experiences with his own parents. My skirmishes with his parents was inciting shame in him as well. He felt it was his duty to make me toe the line, like he had been doing all his life, to keep his parents happy. We were trying to fix each other so that we could escape our shame. This made us get into endless fights. We didn't realize that we both were dealing with our own shame, and acting as victims.

During my meditation practice and counselling sessions, I realized what was making me feel the shame. I realized that the tone and the words that my in-laws used were the same that my parents and teachers had used with me when I was young. In the culture where I grew up, it was natural for elders to shame the young ones, and I never realized how I had associated with it. I used to feel very small and unworthy when I was shamed as a child. And, it was the same feeling of shame and rejection that was being triggered by my in-laws as well. My husband had learnt to suppress his shame by pleasing his parents. And, on seeing his parent's disappointment in me, he wanted to fix me to resolve the situation. Thus, we criticized each other and created drama day over day for many years.

It's only after we realized that both of us were acting out of shame that we began to heal ourselves. I realized that just because my in-laws were disappointed in me it didn't mean that I was at fault. I decided to discuss the matter with them directly instead of trying to please them and failing every time. And, my husband also realized that he didn't have to fix me to hide his own shame. With this new understanding my husband and I were able to have heartfelt and empathetic discussions with each other and my in-laws. This healed not just our respective shames, but our relationships too.

We're falsely led to believe that there is something wrong with us for which we need to be shamed. I grew up in a culture where shaming was a technique to discipline children. A shame-ridden person is often confused as being well-mannered and humble. But no one deserves to be shamed. It's important to realize that for shame to be healed, it needs to be externalized. You can work through the exercise below to uncover and heal the shame within you.

1. Recall a time from your childhood when you experienced shame because of your caregivers – a feeling that you had to run or hide and quickly cover up from that person or situation.

2. Now observe that situation with detachment. Watch the "little you" feeling vulnerable and shamed, the feelings that you couldn't even comprehend back then. May be you were made to believe that your needs/emotions at that moment didn't matter. Now write down how you felt when that happened.

____

____

3. Consider the fact that your caregivers were incomplete themselves. Rather than shielding and supporting you, they were drawing validity from you. They switched roles. Understanding this now doesn't mean that you have to hold a grudge against them. Remember that they did what they knew best.

4. Accept the abandonment that you felt as a child, and allow yourself to grieve over it. Give yourself some time to cry about it, if you need to.

5. Close your eyes and visualize hugging the little child (yourself). Tell the child that it wasn't her fault. Embrace the little child and let her now that you're there to support them. Accept yourself and your emotions the way you wanted your caregivers to love and accept you.

6. Try a useful technique that can bring your private self and external self together. It's called the "mirror technique". Shame is about hiding away from the world. But shame-based people need to express themselves to the external world to heal themselves. Look at yourself in the mirror and accept your life, situations, feelings, body type, face, intelligence, success, etc. Do this repeatedly until you feel synced with yourself. Acknowledge that you felt insecure, left-out, unsupported, unaccepted, and hurt. Accept how your life got out of control because of your habit of hiding your true self from the world.

7. Try and understand which of your actions were really mistakes and which of those were just notional mistakes based on what your family values taught you. For

example, there might have been a family rule where you were not allowed to express your thoughts and emotions if they were different from that of the elders.

____

____

8. Learning to be intimate with others is an important step for a shame-based person so that they can open up about their private selves. It is important to expose your mistakes, defeats, and hurts to a trustworthy person in a safe way, but not as a victim, rather as facts. If you feel ashamed about revealing your true self, take it as a literal challenge so that you can reunite the split halves of yourselves. Write down the name of a person(s) with whom you would like to share your private self.

____

____

The greatest wound shame-based people carry in their hearts is not having an intimate relationship with their partners. Since they are putting up a façade to save themselves, they can't be honest. So they play games, play the victim card, and cut off emotionally. This person's partner will constantly feel distant from her and will remain dissatisfied in their relationship. This relationship is doomed. But it's time to be one with your significant other. Write down a few lines that will come in handy when you express your vulnerability to your partner.

____

____

9. As shame-based people never had anyone to depend on in their childhood, they don't know how to develop trust and dependency. All they have experienced are relationships based on abandonment. It is highly likely that they will bring the same into all their relationships, including in that with their partners. If they work on building trust and dependency with their partners, little by little, they will begin to experience healthy relationships. Write down a few areas where you can start depending upon your partner.

____

____

10. Shame-based people will experience shame by looking at other's successes and achievements. They will not be able to express genuine appreciation for them. It's important that they learn to embrace their own and other's uniqueness, and not compare. Write down the names of a few people with whom you compare yourself, and in what areas. How much are you ready to let go of this habit and express genuine appreciation?

____

____

11. Plan for the next time your triggers are pulled. Plan what you will do and say to convey your feelings without accepting the shame. For example, if someone tries to shame you for spending money on expensive clothes, you can say, "I understand that you like to spend your money in a certain way. But rewarding myself with good clothes makes me happy." Write down a few handy lines to show your vulnerability and express your emotions truly. Remember to be courteous.

____

____

For shame-based people, spiritual awakening is impossible as they don't know which is their true self, the one they project or the one they suppress. Until the externalization work is done, it is impossible to reunite your split self and become a whole. When you learn to accept yourself and others, you will have more meaningful relationships, and move towards spiritual awakening.

CHAPTER 10

BOUNDARIES Set You free!

"Good fences make good neighbors." – Robert Frost

Healthy boundaries are the limits we set up physically, emotionally, and mentally. Boundaries are not built with an ego-centric point of view, but from a strong understanding of the self. A deeper understanding of yourself helps you define your limits better. Boundaries can have a negative connotation in our mind. At one end of the spectrum is a person who keeps others at arm's length, has a big NO written all over his face, and is inconsiderate to others. This person lives in a lonely fortress with high impenetrable walls. At the other end of the spectrum is a person who has no concept of boundaries, doesn't know when to say no, and doesn't realize that they are abusing others, and are getting abused by letting others intrude in theirs matters. In this day and age of social media, the concept of boundaries is further reduced as we're now habitually oversharing our lives with our family, friends, and even strangers. A person with no concept of boundaries is like a horse-rider who has no control over the horse, and lets the horse run without direction, and is depending on the horse's instinct to take him to his destination. Healthy boundaries help us define some safe limits around us, which keep our emotions safe, and yet let us engage with others effectively.

A person first learns about boundaries in his interactions with his parents as a child. Unhealthy boundaries in a parent-child relationship may reflect one or many of the following traits:

- **Parents do for their child what she can do herself**. Even when a child is very young, she is capable of performing some tasks like eating, dressing, washing up, cleaning after herself, etc. And, as the child grows into an adolescent and teenager, she becomes increasingly capable of making decisions and taking care of herself. Intrusive parents who don't maintain boundaries like to have a say in almost everything in their child's life, which stifles the child's sense of identity.

- **Taking decision for them without understanding** their emotions, feelings, or asking for their consent. Since this child relies on her parents' decisions (willingly or unwillingly), it makes the child feel incompetent about making her own decisions.

- **Interrogating**. Parents can get overinvolved in their child's life by asking for the minutest of details without maintaining boundaries. This doesn't leave room for the child to become independent.

- **Intimidating** your children with punishments or threats. For example, saying things like, "Let your father come, I'll tell him what you did," or "If you don't finish your homework, you won't get dessert."

- **Showing over concern.** Parents may overreact to every little accident or incident in their own lives or that of their child. The child will start hiding from her parents to avoid their overwhelming reactions.

- **Not respecting the personal space** of your kids, or your kids not respecting that of yours. For example, when you enter your child's room without knocking, your child learns to do the same. I'd like to give an example of a close friend of mine. When he was a child, it was considered rude to lock his room. When he was married he was having an intimate moment with his wife. When his father knocked on the door, he got overwhelmed and impulsively opened the door, even when his wife was half-naked.

- **Making kids the focus.** If the couple doesn't develop a boundary around them as a single unit, the kids will rule the divided parents. What they can't get from the mother, they'll try to get it by manipulating the father.

- **Oversharing details about your life** with your children, also called emotional parentification. Parents need emotional maturity to stop themselves from sharing every details about their life, like financial distress, marital issues, issues with relatives and friends, with their children. A child needs a safe and secure space to flourish, and doesn't need to know about adult problems. Oversharing confuses the child and makes her feel that she needs to fill her parents' shoes.

- **Treating your child's achievements as your own or letting them identify with your achievements.** Do you rely too much on your child's success to feel good? These parents steal the thunder from their child and don't let them own their achievements and grow from them. On the other hand, a child may develop a false sense of identity when they identify with their parent's success. I had a schoolmate whose father was a famous politician. He felt entitled and superior to other kids because his dad was highly successful.

- **Letting your child have a say in your matters.** When you treat your child as a friend and let them have a say in your matters you give up your parental authority. The question to ask here is am I providing responsibly as a parent or am I allowing my children to make the decision for me? For example, don't let your teen dictate how to maintain your relationship with your husband. If clear lines are not drawn to maintain hierarchy and responsibility, the roles become confused, leading to chaos and eventual hurt.

- **Having no goal of your own.** Do you believe that you are living for your children? I know so many couples who have given up all their goals in life – career, romance, travel, etc., after their kids were born. Parents drawing too much emotional sustenance from their children will most likely invade their space. A parent who may have too much time on her hands may end up over-indulging in the child's life to fulfill her own incomplete wishes.

- **Parents viewing their child as their "little one"** even when they are adults. Narcissistic parents will view the child as a part of themselves to satisfy their own emotional needs. They will keep their kids tied to them, and will not allow the children to transition into adulthood.

- **No detachment in love.** Parents may blur the boundary

between themselves and their children. The child may have aspirations or likings which are different from that of their parents, especially, when the children grow up into adults. It's important for them to take on their own lives, but they can't do so because of their overzealous parents. Over-attached parents can never let the children build their own worlds.

- **Parents and children manipulate each other.** Parents may manipulate the child with emotional blackmail. A child may manipulate the parent by throwing tantrums.

- **Not trusting your children with money.** Parents don't need to keep a tab on the pocket money they give to their children. This habit, if sustained, will lead to the parents keeping a tab on their children's earnings and savings even when they grow up.

All families use these tactics to different degrees. It's best if you look at the tactics you use, and make amends. A family which lacks structure and discipline, and is ridden with vices like overprotection, control, ugly marital conflict, no sense of identity and responsibility, blame and criticism leads to the unhealthy development of a child. A child who is the product of such an upbringing is depressed, anxiety-prone, angry, shame- and guilt-ridden. She is a "lost child". When this lost child grows up and gets married, she involves her parents in her marriage as a "third wheel", letting them have a say in her emotions and decisions, and leaning on them for support. History repeats itself, and this person will most likely create the same childhood for her children as she doesn't know any better. On the other hand, secure attachment promotes cognitive, emotional, and social development with a strong sense of identity and self.

The genesis of a family is rooted in the relationship of the couple. A strong relationship between the couple is necessary to sustain an environment where all family members can thrive. Unhealthy boundaries between the couple can take one or more of the following colors:

- **When an individual's self-identity is not formed before marriage,** she may still be relying on her parents or siblings to help her make decisions. So, the couple will end up having a confused relationship where they will not be able to unite as one.

- **Not knowing how to differentiate between needs, desires, and wishes.** The focus in a couple's relationship should be on needs (material, physical, emotional, and spiritual needs) and not on desires and wishes. It's only when you're clear about your needs can you communicate the same to your spouse in a healthy manner. The focus should not be on your own needs only. It's important to understand the needs of your partner as well, and work towards fulfilling it.

- **Inability to own up to your flaws and openly talk about it.** In our relationships, we can either be too rigid or we can be flimsy and say "sorry" without meaning it. In both the situations, we're superficial, and we're not building the relationship with trust and honesty. Being vulnerable and responsible for our words and actions help us connect with our partners better.

- **Abusing each other emotionally, verbally, and physically.** I need not say anything more about it. It's self-explanatory how all boundaries are breached traumatically here.

- **Speaking negatively about your spouse,** or giving negative signals, in front of your children, family, and friends. This is a breach of confidentiality in a couple's relationship where the trust is broken. The other person will not be able to bond intimately.

- **Allowing others to talk negatively about your spouse.** Not standing up for your spouse in front of your family, friends, and society creates the feeling of betrayal and resentment. Once this happens, it will take a lot of effort to build the trust again.

- **Ignoring your spouse,** not remembering your promises, however small they maybe, gives out a signal to your spouse that they are insignificant. For example, simple tasks like cleaning out the garage, going to the church with them, preparing dinner, celebrating occasions, can all be important. These small instances contribute to the overall feeling of well-being in a family on a daily basis.

- **Withdrawing from your spouse.** Taking differences personally and withdrawing can create a big wall between a couple. Learning how to manage these differences amicably is very important for creating healthy boundaries.

- **Unhealthy communication** involving criticism, blame, stonewalling, and defensiveness promotes a hostile, closed relationship, where the personal boundaries are not respected.

- **Unhealthy conflict resolution** means making the other person give into your idea without understanding and collaboration. This will breed anger and resentment in the relationship.

- **Misplaced priorities.** Not giving your spouse the priority by setting limits with children, social engagements, work, parents, gadgets, and social media is harmful for a relationship.

- **Assuming and filling the gaps, and not staying curious.** After living with a person for a while, we assume that we know them in and out. We box them within our perceptions. We often say things like, "I know where this is going," or "I know what you're thinking," or "I know what you will do next." This kills the possibility for something new to occur. And even when it happens, we crucify it with our thoughts.

- **Unhealthy expectations** of "should", "must", and "have". Words like, "As a husband, you should …," or "As a wife, you must…," or "You just have to…" These parameters are hurtful, and create defenses which will never let you come close to your significant other. Life will steer you in different directions, leading to fights on insignificant matters.

- **Disloyalty** of any kind, including harmless flirting, creates insecurity, mistrust, and anxiety in a relationship. Therefore, having complete transparency in all matters allows trust to occur and flourish. Trust is not something that can be demanded, it has to be earned. You have to be open and vulnerable in order to build trust. Simple everyday acts of transparency, especially, where you know your partner is insecure, will help you build trust. Trust cannot be developed overnight; it takes time, patience, and persistence to breed.

We generally know when our boundaries are getting breached, but we're too afraid to enforce them because of the insecure relationship we may have with the other person. Creating boundaries doesn't mean that one has to be harsh, thorny, aggressive, or authoritative. This makes you an unapproachable and hostile person. Also remember, boundaries are not set in stone. They are constantly evolving. And, none of the boundaries can be termed as right or wrong; you have to decide what works best for you at that point in your life. Boundaries are built from a deeper understanding of yourself and others. By being honest and clear in your communication about your boundaries, you can create a secure, happy, and interdependent relationship that is not rooted in fear, shame, guilt, and authority. Respecting your own boundaries and that of others go hand in hand. For example, if you don't want people to yell at you, you can't yell at them either. If you hold your personal space sacred, you can't breach that of others.

People these days are struggling with work-life balance, long working hours, long commutes, financial needs, etc. It's all work and no play. Our work lives and personal lives are very tightly connected, and it's important to set boundaries in your work life in order to "have a life". These are some of the ways in which we let our work overpower our lives:

- **Decisions at work impact your personal life.** I understand that it's exciting to be offered that new position or promotion. However, before latching on to work opportunities in your life, it's important to consider all the consequences of your choices. Not all opportunities may come in a holistic package.

- **Bringing work or work-related stress at home** interferes with the boundaries of your family and your own health. People who are married can see a direct impact of their work stress on their relationship with their spouse and kids. When we're young and filled with ambition, we may not give attention to our personal growth and our health, and burn out at work. Not enjoying our lives at every stage will result in a mid-life crisis.

- **Getting embroiled in workspace competition** makes us lose focus of our original goals that made us take up the job in the first place.

- **Letting words and actions of superiors and colleagues affect our mood.** It's important to create an external boundary to not let this happen to us. Many organizations these days have strong anti-harassment policies, and it's important to make use of these facilities. Apart from creating an external boundary, take care of your mental peace as well. What others think about you doesn't define you. There are many apps that help you meditate, or let you punch your boss virtually!

- **Giving too much importance to work.** We can get consumed by our work in the fear of losing in the rat race. This doesn't let us lower our guard even when we're not at work, leading us to have mental issues and incomplete relationships.

- **Setting too much expectations on yourself and others.** It's important to know your own limits, and set realistic goals. Learn how to say no to extra work.

- **Not knowing how to manage your time effectively.** Having a timetable, and the discipline to follow it goes a long way in managing everyday stress. Avoid procrastinating and doing things at the last moment. When you're pressed for time while completing a project, it's natural to be stressed and ignore other things that matter in life. Plan ahead so that you can complete your projects in time and don't wait for them to become urgent.

- **Being too available for others.** Investigate the urgency of someone's request before agreeing to help them. Remember you may have urgent tasks of your own. I had a colleague who would come to my desk for help every now and then. Every time he came to me, I thought it would be just a small discussion. But in reality, they would take much longer than I thought, eating away precious time from my schedule. I later learnt to investigate how urgent his task was, and if I was too busy, I would direct him to someone else.

- **Not able to manage priorities.** Not everything is

urgent. Many of us live in a frenzied state of urgency without realizing that some things can wait till later. You can squeeze in time to attend your kid's football match or recital, or steal a lunch with your wife. You don't have to go crazy because of work.

- **Turning money and work into your identity.** Many men derive their identity and self-worth from money and success. This is very damaging for relationships since all their thoughts, ideas, and decisions are focused on making money.

- **Unhealthy management of stress.** Not taking enough breaks or time-off, drinking too much caffeine, smoking, eating junk during work are all unhealthy ways of managing stress.

While it is important to build boundaries, we need to be clear what the boundaries are for and why we are creating them. Simply being averse to outside influence and saying "no" is not creating boundaries, it is creating walls. It might be easy to mistake boundaries as rigid, impermeable walls. Erecting walls around yourself only keeps everyone away from you. Walls create barriers, not boundaries. I know setting healthy boundaries is a challenge for many.

Before you begin to create boundaries, it is very important to know yourself. Answer each question below as it pertains to you.

1. What makes me create this boundary?

    a. Beliefs and values

    b. My personality and that of others (boundaries will

differ from person to person)

2. Why is it important for me?

   a. What am I trying to protect, painful emotions of guilt, shame, and past experiences?

   b. What do I gain or what do I lose by making this boundary?

3. What made me define this limit?

   a. Investigating inaccurate information

4. What are the effects on me and on others around me?

Boundaries are not just for people around you; they are also meant to set your own limits. How much time do you want to spend on your phone, work, relationships, household chores, self-care? Are you creating boundaries to exert power over others? If your boundaries don't respect yourself and others, it will antagonize people around you.

Boundaries are to –

- Improve our relationships
- Allow openness and vulnerability
- Conserve energy
- Feel healthy
- Respect other's boundaries and feelings
- Accept and own up to our mistakes
- Not for manipulating others
- Evolve with time
- Made with emotions, not just logic

- Satisfy needs, not wants and desires
- Never right or wrong, they just are

Healthy boundaries let you talk from your feelings. It's no one's responsibility if you felt bad or good about something. Express your feelings in terms of your own emotions, and not to point fingers or to control others[1] . The example below explains that.

I feel ___________ when ___________. I need ______________.

I feel SAD/ANGRY/GUILTY/ASHAMED/GLAD/MAD when I'm spoken to like this. I need us to have an empathetic conversation instead of yelling.

vs.

You're rude, you always talk to me like this. What have I done to deserve this? Next time be respectful when you talk to me.

Boundaries have a different meaning, understanding, and visual for each of us. Boundaries come under four major categories which are physical, emotional, intellectual, and sexual.

Physical: It is the physical distance you allow other people to maintain with you. The concept of physical boundary is especially important with people who were once your caregivers as it is with them that you learnt the concept of boundaries. As a child, if your personal boundary was breached, your gut feeling would have told you so. You might have felt repulsed, but shame took over and made

---

[1]It's important to mention that if you or someone in your family is struggling with trauma, depression, or BPD, then it needs support from a therapist or specialist.

you submit to their abuse (intentional / unintentional).

Physical boundary has multiple levels –

- Proximity: It is the physical closeness you allow someone to maintain with you. Showing affection with an occasional hug or a kiss is fine, but being physically close to someone (other than your spouse) habitually is unnatural.

- Touch: How your parents touched you when you were growing up is very important, and it determines how you tolerate abuse even in the future.

  - Early childhood: After five-six years of age, parents may still bathe their children, touch their private parts, help them put on clothes, make them sit on their lap, etc. This is breaching the personal space of a child.

  - Puberty: When children become aware of their sexuality, it is unwarranted to kiss and hug them, except occasionally. It is also not healthy to share the same bed with them.

  - Teenage: When your child has reached this stage, they need to be given the same respect as you would give to an adult.

- Personal space: It is respecting the privacy of someone's room, closet, and belongings. It is especially important to maintain this boundary at the time when your child has reached puberty. It is important to let your child make their beds, fold their clothes, and tidy their rooms. This entitles them with a sense of responsibility, ownership, and boundary.

Emotional: This simply means respecting the emotions of others.

- Taking responsibility for your emotions: It is important to manage your emotions yourself and share only what is important. Once you start to overshare your emotions with someone, it becomes a slippery slope. Before you know, you have become an emotional burden on someone. On the other hand, forcing someone to share their emotions with you is also a breach of their boundary. Like everything else, emotional boundaries are especially important in a parent-child relationship. It's important to build a relationship based on trust where someone can share their emotions powerfully and responsibly.

- Respecting emotions of others: Parents may be too busy and distracted in their lives which makes them emotionally unavailable to their children. When children share emotions with their parents, they may shrug it off as something "silly", "stupid", or "cute". These children may grow up to think that their emotions don't matter, and will learn to be subservient to their parents and to others. Everybody's emotions, irrespective of age, are important and should be treated with respect.

Intellectual: When someone shares their ideas and reasoning, it is important to give them a patient ear. It doesn't simply mean pretending, but rather actively listening to what they are trying to convey. This also means not arguing and proving that your point is better than theirs. Not giving someone a space to express their intellectual thoughts is breaching their intellectual boundary. Even though we may belong to the same blood family, but we're all intellectually different. We see this being violated every day in many settings. Be it news channel debates, where people are busy screaming over others without consideration, or in social gatherings, office settings, and dining room discussions.

Financial: In this day and age, money has the power to make you feel in control and creates a sense of independence. It is important to respect the financial boundaries of your spouse and children. Everyone has the right to personal property, and it should never be violated.

Sexual: An appropriate distance needs to be maintained to ensure that the child's private parts are not accidently touched or caressed. This also extends to unintentional contact with breast or penis when giving a loving and benign hug. Nudity at home, like changing clothes in front of each other, handling each other's undergarments, is intrusion of sexual space. Inappropriate remarks passed at home about someone else's body, especially private parts, is also crossing sexual boundaries. Keeping gender-based biases in a family such as "men don't cry" or "girl's need to look pretty" make your children uncomfortable about expressing their sexuality.

Boundaries, or lack thereof, are first established/ experienced with your immediate blood relations (parents and siblings). Only when you have created healthy boundaries with them can you extend it to somebody else, including your partner and children.

1. Barring your basic needs of food, shelter, and clothes, describe how you rely on the following people for your needs (what are you getting and not getting): physical, emotional, intellectual, and financial.

Relationship	Needs being met	Needs not being met
Mother		
Father		
Siblings		

2. Write down how "rigid or fragile" your boundaries are with the following people. Rigid boundaries are those which are impermeable like a brick wall. Fragile boundaries, on the other hand, are the ones which can be broken/ violated any time. Healthy boundaries are usually those which lie in the middle.

Relationship	Physical	Emotional	Intellectual	Financial	Sexual
Mother					
Father					
Siblings					

3. If you had to recreate boundaries with your family, write down how healthy boundaries would look like with each of the relations below.

Relationship	Physical	Emotional	Intellectual	Financial	Sexual
Mother					
Father					
Siblings					

4. Write down specific actions you can take to convert your unhealthy boundaries into healthy ones. For example, if someone in your family is passing an inappropriate remark, how will you counter them to establish a healthy boundary? Remember shame and guilt may arise when you're trying to set these new boundaries. See below a couple of examples about how you can set and reinforce boundaries with others effectively.

Effective	Ineffective
I feel violated when you enter my room behind me. I value privacy. I need to keep my things the way I want to, without feeling insecure that someone will enter my room behind me. Next time onwards, please don't enter when I'm not present.	KEEP OUT OF MY ROOM!! How many times have we had this discussion?
I feel overwhelmed when you ask me too many questions and keep a tab on everything that happens in my life. I need time and space to evaluate what I'm comfortable sharing with you.	YOU HAVE MADE MY LIFE HELL!! I run from you to avoid your stalking.

People who lack boundaries have a high level of neediness (desperate need of attention and validation). They choose to compromise their identity and remove all boundaries. They are very susceptible to receiving abuse and inflicting abuse as they have no idea about how to respect other's spaces. Write down how you will reinforce boundaries when they are not being respected even though you tried to set them up.

You're creating a boundary	Them (who you are creating it with)	You (reinforcing)
I love this girl, we have been dating for a long time. I want to marry her. I want you to know that she is of a different religion. I hope you will love and respect her too.	Parents: They show disapproval by non-verbal cues like facial expressions, eye rolls, and gestures. Verbally they say, "How you've shamed all of us! I thought we had taught you well. We had sacrificed so much for you, and this is what we get in return? You will not have a happy marriage because we're different. You must listen to us." This incites shame and guilt.	I can understand how you feel. I want you to know that I really love her, and she loves me too. She is an amazing girl, and I couldn't have found anybody better than her. I will marry her. Her religion doesn't bother me, and mine doesn't bother her. I hope you will be able to love and respect her as you love and respect me.
Please knock on the door before entering my room. And if I don't answer, please don't just enter. Sometimes I forget to lock the door, but a shut door means I need privacy.	Family: Not everyone is respecting your boundary yet, and some people still don't knock before entering. They still haven't understood your need for privacy, and continue bothering you with unimportant and frequent interruptions.	Please respect my space. I have been saying this for a while now. Disturb me only when it's important. I have bought this "DONOT DISTURB" sign, and when you see this hanging on the door knob, don't even knock. Don't feel shame or guilt in establishing this boundary with your family. This doesn't define your love for them. Any change in the family system is not easy. But when you're clear and persistent, a new life experience begins.

CHAPTER 11

I, Me, Myself – SELF-CARE

"You can't pour from an empty cup." – Norm Kelly

Self-care simply means self–you — and care –deliberate or intentional effort to maintain/protect yourself in all aspects on a daily basis. People who don't indulge in self-care on a daily basis lead a mechanical, reactive, robotic, angry, and dissatisfied life. While living a reactive life day in and day out, we eventually lose connection with ourselves. And, we can't understand our dissatisfaction. Our relationships suffer, sleep patterns are disrupted (45% of us lay awake at night as per some recent surveys), and we develop unhealthy eating habits. How many of us live this kind of a monotonous life? Our lives resemble a sergeant's drill where we're doing the exact same things, having the same thoughts, and feeling the same emotions day after day. We get up at exactly the same time, on the same side of the bed, brush and bathe in the same exact way, commute to our work on the same route, greet our colleagues the same way, have the same work experiences, crib the same way about our work and bosses, leave from work at the same time, get frustrated about the traffic in the same way, reach home exhausted with the same dull face, and greet our families the same way. Then we sit dazed for a couple of hours until our partners pick up a fight with us, which is also routine. We stay glued to our phones and gadgets for mindless entertainment until it's time to hit the bed, all the while worrying about the next day. And, then we hit the repeat button again as the next day begins. Even if a miracle happened, and God appeared in front of us, I bet, we would still hit the repeat button.

Most of us think that self-care means slowing down and being mindful. But to the contrary, self-care means getting to a place of optimum balance. Take for instance, a talkative person who is quick to speak her mind without thinking about how it would affect other people. Such a person needs to slow down and talk mindfully. But at the same time, a person who doesn't talk, and is numbed, needs to get in touch with herself and her emotions to build her self-esteem and confidence, to connect with others compassionately and empathetically. Self-care, as a concept, was introduced in popular culture during the mid-1900s. Back then, it simply meant physically taking care of yourself and your hygiene–haircuts, bathing, taking care of your look, etc.

Even today self-care is grossly misunderstood in the following ways:

1. **Self-care is selfish**. In many collectivistic cultures, self comes after the family and community. Taking care of yourself is generally looked down upon as being selfish or vain. When you're not taking care of yourself, and not taking responsibility for your emotions, you automatically assign the blame outside. Taking care of other's needs without getting your own needs met can only lead to suppression, frustration, blame, anger, resentment, and revenge. Self-care is like the oxygen mask that you must wear to protect yourself at all times before saving your loved ones.

2. **Self-care is a luxury of time and money,** and some

think that it's a waste and is only for the rich. Wrong. Self-care doesn't mean going on luxurious vacations, using expensive beauty products, eating organic food, buying branded clothes, driving fancy cars, or living in opulent homes. Going on a vacation because everyone else does so is not self-care. It is rather a source of stress because of the money spent and the efforts involved to get acceptance in the social pack because of our herd mentality. According to a survey, 48% of the population thinks self-care is not possible due to lack of time, and 58% believe that self-care is expensive. But, in reality, material possessions have little impact on our overall well-being. I personally indulge in self-care while sitting at home by getting up early in the morning to meditate, going for a morning walk to watch the sunrise, planning healthy meals for the week during the weekends, and joining free online yoga classes. I own a normal home, drive a basic car, and still have great friends. I make it a point to spend quality time with family every day. Self-care doesn't have to cost money.

3. **Self-care is not entertaining ourselves** with TV, social gatherings, dining-out, etc. When we're engaged in mindless entertainment, we're disconnected from our emotions and feelings. At the same time, we're letting the negative pervade our minds through the bombardment of unwanted information. Social gatherings can also be stressful because they call for certain standards that need to be met. Also, lack of acceptance in a social setting can lead to a feeling of

worthlessness. Even though meeting people socially is important, we need to be mindful about choosing (choosing is self-care) the right person to meet, and deciding how much time and energy to invest in them. Not everyone will uplift our emotional energy. Making sure that we're emotionally and mentally uplifted is important, and not selfish. We always have a choice. We're never bound. This applies even for our family members and relatives. I want to stress here that you have a choice of whom you want to interact with, why you want to interact and how much you want to interact. Even if we don't want to disconnect with someone fully, we can maintain a healthy distance from them by forming boundaries. This is self-care. We're all different, even if we have the same blood running through our veins. It's okay to make different choices.

Sometimes taking care of hygiene helps us pick up our lives from the rut, and gets us to a better state of mind. But it is not a fix or a solution. As a concept, self-care has evolved with time, and now it is not just about external hygiene, but also relates to internal and mental hygiene. Insights into who we're, how we feel, how we react, and what we like and dislike help us know ourselves better and help us make better life choices.

Till about the age of twenty-five, I too didn't know the real meaning of self-care. For me, self-care meant wearing good clothes, having a good hairstyle, basically it was all about my appearance. I was very reactive in my emotions, and the concept of mental care was alien to me. Aren't emotions self-generated? How could I control my mental state? In relationships with my friends and family, I had no boundaries. I just went with the flow in any given situation. If I had any negative thoughts about my close ones, I would feel ashamed and guilty. I was at the disposal of others. I was afraid that if I said "no" to someone, they would leave me. My work life was a mess. I was frustrated at work. But I thought it was normal to feel like that about work. My career choices were driven by the need for money and status, and not by my interests or strengths. I couldn't take criticism, however constructive it might have been. I was low in self-esteem and self-confidence, but was in denial about it. I loved to hear and intellectualize empowering thoughts, but when it came to taking actions, there were few. Spirituality for me meant praying and going to a place of worship. But I had no connection with myself or with the universe. It was only after I started my meditation practice did the blinders come off step by step.

I started to de-clutter my mind through meditation. I was no longer operating from a place of remorse for the past or fear of the future. The baggage of unwanted thoughts was removed. I practiced self-love which helped me accept my positives and negatives (see mirror work by Louise L. Hay). I took the help of counsellors and therapists to heal my past emotions and traumas. At the physical level, this helped me accept my body the way it was; I wasn't striving to get the diva-like figure anymore. I started sleeping at 9 a.m. so that I could wake up at 5 a.m. the next day. This gave me time for meditation and morning walks before leaving for work. With this realization of self, I started to choose the people that I wanted to be with. I learnt to create boundaries in my relationships and started dealing with people with compassion, empathy, and forgiveness. I learnt to detach from people, but with love. I continued to keep the relationship, but without getting influenced by the baggage they brought. In my professional life, I started to observe my strengths and weaknesses, and aligned my career choices accordingly. I learnt to leave work at office, and spend quality time with my family. Personal growth took on a different meaning. I became more curious and open to change than ever before. I see a new dimension opening up for me almost every day. I'm amazed at the power I now have to see beyond my limitations, and open up an ocean of possibilities. In my spiritual journey, I can now see a clear demarcation between my emotions, thoughts, and body. I can choose what I want to keep and what I want to let go. Beyond prayers and places of worship, I find spirituality in humanity and in connecting with the universe. I have associated myself with multiple non-profit organizations which are engaged in the ethical treatment of animals, disaster relief, and helping human trafficking survivors.

These days a big hurdle in self-care is multitasking, which has become a part of everyone's life. We're constantly switching from one role to another without giving it a thought. A person who is multitasking can't be mindful of his actions, and often triggers a chain reaction. Consider that you're sitting in office and are stretched too thin. Your spouse calls you to talk about something. Most likely you won't be able to have a mindful conversation with her, leaving her feeling disgruntled. With this mood, she won't be able to attend to her work or to the kids properly. This can quickly become a culture in the family where everyone feels disconnected from each other. Had either of them exercised self-care, the chain reaction could have been broken. Like everything else, we learn the concept of self-care from our families while growing up. As kids, we emulate our parents and caregivers in almost everything. If they came back home from work after a busy day, kicked off their shoes, and sat in front of the idiot box, more likely than not, we would end up doing the same thing to cope with a busy day. Alternatively, if we had seen them meditating, spending quality time with the family, exercising, and taking care of their health, then doing the same activities would have become second nature to us.

What is self-care? Self-care, first, means realizing that your life has many facets–physical, mental, emotional, spiritual, social, professional, and personal. It's important to look at yourself in the mirror and see a clear, undistorted, and holistic image. There is a difference between a projected self and the true self.

The projected self comes from how we want others to perceive us. After years of putting up a false face, we assume that that image is our truth. It has become common these days to believe that everything is within our reach, and that we can switch hats on a whim. It is expected that all of us will be superstars in our own right. We all should have powerful careers, amazing relationships, gorgeous bodies, a huge following on social media, fancy vacations, overachieving children, rich and famous lifestyles. "What's new?" is the common question we ask anyone we meet. We all are under pressure to "have something new" to talk about all the time. We fear getting categorized as "normal people having normal lives", and fear being termed as dull. In the fear of being left out, we try to portray that we have an amazing life with a full spectrum of "bling". But we highly underestimate the effects of living a high-achieving, multitasking life. Though it may look fancy from outside, but this way we're running away from our true selves. We're always taught to cover up for our shortcomings, and this is especially true in families who overhype their children's behavior, strengths, and achievements, while hiding their limitations, weaknesses, and mistakes. They derive a sense of pride when their projected selves get acceptance in society. These children will live in a fool's paradise, and attach to their projected self rather than their true self. They will never know their true needs, and won't accept their own limitations. A client of mine, Max, was a stutterer from birth, and he saw the shame is his parent's eyes whenever he stuttered in a social setting. The parents covered up for him by completing his sentences or diverting attention away from him. They would overhype his achievements, and make sure that everyone thought of him as flawless. Seeing his parent's denial, Max also never learnt to accept his stuttering and became an introvert to avoid bringing shame on his parents. He tried extra hard to get good grades in school, and to get into the sport teams. Max has buried his true self under hundreds of layers, and has disconnected from his vulnerable, true self, and doesn't know how to embrace himself. As a consequence, he has become over-competitive and an over-achiever. He pleases his family, friends, and relatives like a loyal dog. In social settings, he purposely displays his intelligence and achievements in all ways possible. He has no personal and spiritual growth. He lives a life filled with stress and frustration, but doesn't know why he feels that way.

What does the true self look like? It starts by embracing the state we're in right now. It could be our financial/work status, speech impediments, failures, body shape, relationship status, education level, ethnicity, nationality, etc. I know it can be scary to accept your true self. It may seem overwhelming, so we want to fix it quickly or deny it. But I assure you that accepting your true-self is only a bliss that you can offer yourself. It's the most comfortable space that we can offer ourselves. Our decisions will be based on our own strengths and weaknesses, and on an understanding of our uniqueness and natural flair. We will feel one with ourselves, peaceful, calm, freed from ego and pretense, and we will see our inner shackles clearly. A true sense of love and compassion arises, for ourselves and for others. We feel one with the universe, letting go of past experiences. Our relationships get better. Unfortunately, we're unable to live with this feeling all the time. The question is if it is even possible to be our true self at every given moment? I would say that the answer is no. But the good side is that we can begin by shortening the gap between the projected self and true self, until there comes a time when we're living our true self almost every day. True self helps us be open to learning, reforming, creating a new and better outlook, and taking actions, which in turn helps us go deeper and live a better, fulfilling, balanced, creative, and loving life. Our tendency to expect all this from other people and situations reduces, and literally diminishes as we keep growing stronger and stronger internally. We will not be driven by our egos, fears, and insecurities. We will not burn our energy in convincing other people that we're good and worthy of their love. As we keep growing internally, we keep exploring our egos and defenses. The more we get connected to our true self, the easier it is for us to break the pattern and allow compassion for ourselves and for others to arise. We will have our guards down with the people we love. This time we will be connecting to others through our true selves, and not the projected selves. Our true selves are always clear about ourselves and others, and do not get carried away by dramas, influences, and confusions. This helps us align with ourselves and others. This deep sense of clarity will give us peace and balance, and help us create a stronger and more expansive foundation which will lead to a life-changing experience. This will let us be, and we will let others be. This letting go of the external identity that is filled with selfishness, impulsiveness, barriers, ego, material gains, and successes is something we all owe to ourselves.

When we uncover our true self, it will be easy to indulge in self-care for our true self, rather than for the projected self.

Self-care is a way in which we give back to ourselves by releasing everyday pressures, to live a balanced, joyful, satisfying, and complete life.

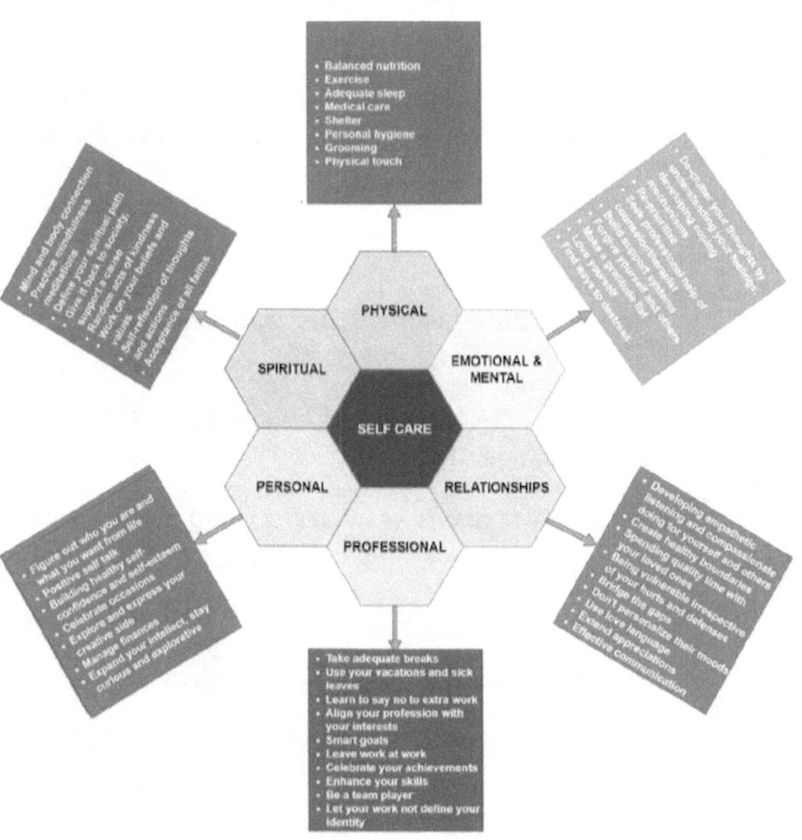
PHYSICAL
SPIRITUAL
EMOTIONAL & MENTAL
SELF CARE
PERSONAL
RELATIONSHIPS
PROFESSIONAL

Balanced nutrition
Exercise
Adequate sleep
Medical care
Shelter
Personal hygiene
Grooming
Physical touch

Mind and body connection
Practice mindfulness
Define your spiritual path
meditations
Give it back to society, support a cause
Random acts of kindness
Work on your beliefs and values
Self-reflection of thoughts and actions
Acceptance of all faiths

Figure out who you are and what you want from life
Positive self talk
Building healthy self, confidence and self-esteem
Celebrate occasions
Explore and express your creative side
Manage finances
Expand your intellect, stay curious and explorative

Developing empathetic, listening and compassionate
doing for yourself and others
Create healthy boundaries
Spending quality time with your loved ones
Being vulnerable irrespective of your hurts and defenses
Bridge the gaps
Don't personalize their moods
Use love language
Extend appreciations
Effective communication

Take adequate breaks
Use your vacations and sick leaves
Learn to say no to extra work
Align your profession with your interests
Smart goals
Leave work at work
Celebrate your achievements
Enhance your skills
Be a team player
Let your work not define your identity

Self-care is a way in which we give back to ourselves by releasing everyday pressures, to live a balanced, joyful, satisfying, and complete life.

Below are some questions that will help you uncover your self-care regime. Answer each question with honesty.

Physical self-care

1. Balanced Nutrition

- Are you eating healthy fruits and vegetables on a daily basis?

- Do you eat freshly cooked home-food rather than outside/canned food?

- How many glasses of water do you drink every day?

- How much caffeine do you intake every day?

- How many cans of soda do you drink every day?

- How many cigarettes do you smoke every day?

2. Exercises

- Do you exercise at least three hours a week (gym/cycling/jogging/yoga/aerobics/sports)?

- Are you prevented from exercising by aches and pain? If yes, how much?

- Do you expend energy in doing strenuous household

work?

3. *Adequate sleep*

- Do you follow the "1 hour – no technology" rule before sleeping?

- Do you sleep for eight hours every day?

- Do you have a relaxing bedtime routine?

- How is your sleep quality?

- Do you feel fresh when you wake up?

- Do you fall asleep easily?

- Do you snore or grind your teeth while sleeping?

4. *Medical Care*

- Do you take your medical care seriously?

- Do you go for regular preventative checkups?

- Are you regular with your medications?

5. Personal Hygiene

- Do you bathe every day?

- Do you brush after meals?

- Do you wash your hands after using the bathroom, and before and after meals?

- Do you wash your clothes frequently?

- Do you work on curing your chronic cosmetic conditions like dandruff, acne, dryness, athlete's foot, etc.?

- Do you use a deodorant?

6. Grooming

- Do you understand your body type and know what suits you – hair style, clothing, etc.?

- Do you visit the barber shop regularly?

- Do you iron your clothes before wearing them?

- Do you pay attention to social etiquette – body posture, speaking (tone of voice, choice of words, humility), mannerisms (burping, slurping, table manners)?

Self-care	Current state (1-10)	Desired state (1-10)	Action plan for the next fourteen days to reach desired state
Balanced nutrition			
Exercise			
Adequate sleep			
Medical care			
Personal hygiene			
Grooming			

Emotional and Mental Self-Care

Emotional and Mental States

Angry	Glad	Sad	Shame	Guilt	Afraid
Furious	Elated	Depressed	Sorrow	Regret	Terrified
Enraged	Excited	Agonized	Remorse	Anxiety	Horrified
Outraged	Overjoyed	Alone	Defamed	Low self-	Scared stiff
Boiling	Thrilled	Hurt	Worthless	esteem	Petrified
Irate	Exuberant	Dejected	Disgraced	Depression	Fearful
Seething	Ecstatic	Hopeless	Condemned	Self-harm	Panicky
Loathsome	Fired-up	Sorrowful	Humiliated	Apologetic	Frantic
Betrayed	Passionate	Miserable	Dishonored	Uncomfortable	Shocked
Upset	Cheerful	Heartbroken	Mortified	Self-doubt	Apprehensive
Mad	Gratified	Heartbroken	Admonished	Repentance	Frightened
Defensive	Good	Lost	Unworthy	Compunction	Threatened
Frustrated	Relieved	Distressed	Sneaky	Unscrupulous	Insecure
Agitated	Satisfied	Let down	Embarrassed	Penitence	Uneasy
Disgusted	Glowing	Melancholic	Self-conscious	Atonement	Intimidated
Perturbed	Happy	Unhappy	Secretive	Contrition	Cautious
Annoyed	Contented	Moody	Bashful		Nervous
Uptight	Pleasant	Blue	Ridiculous		Worried
Resistant	Tender	Upset	Outlandish		Timid
Irritated	Pleased	Disappointed	Pitied		Unsure
Touchy	Mellow	Dissatisfied	Silly		Anxious

The list given above mentions the basic emotions that all of us feel in our everyday lives.

We discussed in previous chapters how we can express ourselves in terms of our own feelings (owning up). Most of us label our emotions as "good" or "bad". This chart will help you discover and understand the subtle difference between all the emotions we go through. You can use the exact words mentioned here to express yourself. For example, I feel <u>disgrace</u> when I do things my way, which my family doesn't approve of. I feel <u>terrified</u> to make decisions for myself. I feel very <u>uptight</u> and <u>resistant</u> when the topic of money is discussed.

Knowing our emotional states can help us in monitoring our emotions and centering them.

Pick up any area or situation from the self-care diagram given above, and mark all the emotions that come to you in that situation. This will help you pinpoint where you stand emotionally. Now you can chart a plan to achieve balance with the help of a counsellor, therapist, coach, mentor, or even by yourself. If you work on self-care using this method, you will eventually end up living a very fulfilling life with support, self-confidence, and self-esteem. This can potentially shift your life by 180°, and you will be amazed by the results.

Relationships

Relationships are the most important part of our lives. They are the pillars that support us. Relationships can be with oneself, other people, and even with inanimate objects like cars, homes, gadgets, and with our circumstances like profession, education, social status, etc.

Below are some thought-provoking questions that you can ask yourself about your relationships:

• Do you create drama in your relationships, or are you balanced?

- How frequently do you lose your temper with others?

- What emotions come to you in your relationship? Pick the precise emotions from the six broad categories.

- Is the relationship still needed, or are you carrying it as a baggage? – Unfollow/Unfriend

- How are you benefiting in this relationship?

- Do you feel supported in this relationship, and, if yes, then how?

- What are you bringing to the relationship?

- Do you walk on egg shells in this relationship?

- Do others walk on egg shells around you?

- Do you maintain healthy boundaries in your relationships?

- Do you accept others for who they are, or do you expect unfair things from them?

- Do you remain curious in your relationships, or are you shut down?

- Do you bring your true self in the relationship?

- Do you take ownership of your actions in your relationships, or do you blame and criticize?

- Are you vulnerable in your relationships, or are you defensive?

- Are you actively nurturing the relationship?

- Are you developing empathetic listening and compassionate actions in your relationships every day?

Once you have achieved an insight into a particular relationship, 50% of the work is already done. Now chart out precisely what actions can be taken to develop a healthy balance in the relationship. Think in terms of yourself, without controlling others and expecting anything from them.

Relationship	Name of people involved	Current state (1: un-balanced -10: balanced)	Desired state (1: un-balanced -10: balanced)	Action plan for the next fourteen days to reach desired state
Spouse				
Parents				
Siblings				
Relatives				
Relatives				
Profession				
Colleagues				

Professional

- How do you feel about your work life?

- What are the feelings you carry about your co-workers?

- What kind of a relationship do you have with your boss?

- How do you feel about your skill set?

- When was the last time you learnt a new skill?

- Is your line of work aligned with your strengths?

- Are you a team player?

- Do you set realistic goals?

- Are you competitive with your colleagues?

- Do you help your co-workers without wanting any acknowledgement?

- What is your relationship with money?

- What do you think about money?

- Do you enjoy your wealth?

- How well do you manage your finances?

- Do you switch off notifications after work?

- Do you over-complain about your work to your family members or spouse?

- What score would you give to your work life balance on a scale of 1 (good) -5 (bad)?

In what area would you like to change/ grow?	Where do you think you stand now?	Explore the different choices available / action steps	Resources available	Roadblocks

Personal

Think about each of these questions for at least a minute and then answer.

- Are you moody/emotional or numb/disconnected?

- How high on motivation do you remain throughout the day?

- How frustrated, irritated, snappy, or cynical do you remain throughout the day?

- Are you operating mostly out of your insecurities and fears?

- What holds you back?

- Do you accept your weaknesses as much as your strengths? What can you do to unite them?

- How creative are you on a weekly basis?

- How much do you stand up to your promises?

- Do you surprise your family with weekend meals, getaways, gifts, etc.?

- Do you express your love and kindness?

- How romantic are you in actions?

- Do you keep a gratitude journal?

- Do you celebrate your occasions, achievements, or milestones in any way?

- Have you gone for therapy? We all need it.

- De-clutter three things which are not needed anymore from each area – wardrobe, drawers, kitchen, habits, and past experiences.

- When was the last time you had a good cry?

- When was the last time you punched a bag or a pillow to release pent-up frustration and anger?

- Assign one day of the week as a "no complain day".

- Think about two areas in which you have the strong urge to be perfect, or look good in front of others.

- Think about three harmful things that you do habitually. Are you ready to change these? If yes, write down alternative actions.

- Think about the last week, and mark your stress level out of five.

- What did you learn from your last mistake? What amends did you make for it?

Spiritual

- Introspect on your daily behavior and lifestyle.

- What do you think is your life's purpose?

- What are your operating principles in life? How did you acquire them? Are they fitting into your life right now? If not, how would you like to change them?

- Are you being honest with yourself about everything?

- How much do you experience yourself? In what areas do you experience heavy emotions?

- Have you done your inner healing?

- How much do you live in the present? Are you aware of your surroundings most of the times?

- Have you united your mind and body? If not, how can you do so?

- Do you accept that the mind and body affect each other?

- Do you accept the signals your body gives you?

- Practice mindful breathing, walking, eating, and sitting.

- What would a regret-free life look like?

- Write down four triggers that make you feel shame, blame, angry, and sadness?

- Chart out two areas where you need to tune into your vibrations, and two areas to tune out from.

- Follow a ritual to start your day positively.

- Do you sit in silence without doing or touching anything for fifteen minutes every day?

- Watch the clouds pass-by, star-gaze, or listen to the whistling of leaves for at least twenty minutes.

- Get your hands dirty in soil.

- Do you connect with nature daily, away from the distraction of your gadgets?

- Sponsor a child or a pet.

- Volunteer in a non-profit organization to give back to society.

CHAPTER 12

Don't Believe All your BELIEFS

"Your beliefs become your thoughts. Your thoughts become your words. Your words become your actions. Your actions become your habits. Your habits become your values. Your values become your destiny." - Mahatma Gandhi

We go about our lives guided by an inner voice which helps us make decisions at every step. This inner voice guides us in choosing between right or wrong, moral or immoral, good or bad. In our everyday lives, the spectrum of possible choices available to us at any given point of time is just too large. Our inner voice helps us subconsciously narrow down the possible list of choices. This voice is nothing but our beliefs and values. Beliefs are the set of thoughts that we hold to be true, whereas values are the beliefs that we hold to be important. What we hold as our value is subjective, and differs from one person to the other; we all have different values. The combination of our beliefs and values is our "belief system" which defines our attitude and shapes our personality, behavior, life choices, and our entire future. Everything that we perceive is being filtered through our belief system, which acts like the police to keep us in check. When a group of people start to agree on a set of beliefs and values, it becomes the culture in a family, an organization, and society at large. From a scale of 0-10, assign a value to the following beliefs:

1. Parents deserve to be revered like God. **VALUE:**

2. Money can be earned only with hard work. **VALUE:**

3. Destiny controls my life. **VALUE:**

4. I'm fat, no one will date me. **VALUE:**

5. Men are the providers, and women are the nurturers. **VALUE:**

Higher the value assigned to a belief, greater is the call for action in compliance with the belief. If you assigned a high value to (1), your life will be circling around your parent's choices and decisions. Subconsciously, you will be carrying the same belief structure as theirs, and you won't be able to discover who you are. On the other hand, if this belief is assigned a low value, it's likely that you will be an independent and free-willed individual. A high value against (2) means you will intentionally choose career paths which are the most arduous. You're likely to have rigid financial beliefs, and will not be able to spend it freely. A low value, on the other hand, means you're careless about your work, and you're not able to give in concrete efforts. A high value against (3) means you will not take responsibility for your successes and failures. A low value, on the other hand, means you're over-controlling your life, and you blame yourself every time you fail in an endeavor. A high value against (4) means you have extremely low self-confidence and self-esteem, and are not able to approach the person you really like. A high value against (5) means men are not nurturing towards their families, and women don't place importance on their careers and self-growth.

While growing up I believed that I was not good enough, and this was playing up in all areas of my life. I was an introvert in school, and didn't have a voice of my own.

I was a people-pleaser, too afraid to express my opinions. I didn't think I had anything valuable to contribute in class or in conversations with friends and family. I would mostly remain quiet. When someone spoke to me rudely, I thought I was at fault. This would bring out the people-pleaser in me even further. I could see good qualities in others, but not in myself. Others' achievements seemed too great, praise-worthy, and grandiose, but at the same time, my achievements felt insignificant, unworthy, and boring. If someone praised me for my achievements, it seemed like a pretense, as if they were throwing me a bone and doing me a favor. It's only later in life did I realize that I was being harsh towards myself in thinking so lowly about myself. But the germ of this negative belief lay in my upbringing. I was conceived within a few months of my parents' marriage. When I was born, they were still trying to settle down. So, they grew overprotective about me since I was their first child, and wouldn't let me make my own decisions. But my grandmother favored by younger sister over me. As a child I couldn't assess my own complex emotions, and the only thing I believed was that there was something wrong in me.

When we're born, we're closely aligned to our instincts. However, as we keep growing we absorb the beliefs propagated by our families, schools, and the society. When we're young, we're very curious about our existence and about the world. We're soaking up knowledge like a sponge, without much questioning. We implicitly believe everything that our parents tell us. Moreover, the way we assign importance to our beliefs mirrors that of our family. Slowly we learn to block our instincts and intuitions, and become more like people around us. And just like them, we jump to conclusions quickly, and judge the situations in our lives. Instead of staying curious, we find comfort in relying on the common beliefs in our families. Families think of these common beliefs as their "family heritage" which is passed on from one generation to the next. This family heritage becomes the "covenant of truth" that all members must live by. This forces all members to think alike, which then becomes a common source of identity. And, this guides our actions and interactions with the outside world. Another set of beliefs and values that are acquired are the result of personal experiences. Yet another factor that determines beliefs and value is society—the popular culture prevailing at that time. Thus, our core values are, by and large, imposed upon us by our families, our personal experiences, and our culture. Now culture can change drastically from one geographical area to another, and evolve over time. The eastern culture gives more importance to the family in contrast to the western culture. People in smaller towns and cities give more importance to rest and recreation as compared to that in busy metropolitan cities. A century earlier, the equality of women was not considered important. The value you assign to a belief also depends on your circumstances. If your livelihood depends on oil drilling, you're less likely to support environmental policies.

Beliefs are the web we live in. All our choices, big or small, are dictated by our beliefs. Our lives can become either heaven or hell based on the beliefs that we're caged in. Our core beliefs, which are largely shaped by our early childhood, formulate our self-image. A powerful self-image makes us feel confident, and humble, and helps us connect with people without victimizing ourselves or others. Alternatively, an underwhelming self-image makes us feel incapable, and keep us riddled in self-doubt, thereby making us feel like victims. Thoughts like, "People make fun of me," or "I'm not good enough and I will never succeed," are common in such cases. A negative self-image makes us put too much emphasis on how we're perceived in society, and engage with other people in an unhealthy way. Then the source of our self-image becomes external. Thereby, it influences the kind of homes we live in, the types of cars we drive, the clothes we wear, the career choices we make, or the people we date. This makes us lose our focus on what really matters. It makes us prioritize a high-paying job and career growth over a chance to spend quality time with our families. It makes us give more importance to social obligations than to our emotional needs and those of our families. On the other hand, someone who gives importance to interpersonal relationships is more likely to be a considerate person capable of being vulnerable to others. Such a person will not be running after acceptance and external validation.

When I was in school I was really very interested in the subject of psychology. I would devour books on psychology, and dream about becoming a famous psychologist someday, and perhaps making a couple of breakthroughs in the field. I took up psychology as my major during college, and did exceedingly well. However, when time came to start working, I realized that psychology was not a lucrative career choice in my country. Most of my peers were either opting to pursue MBA programs or were entering the corporate world. None of them were pursuing psychology as a career. Instead of following my heart, I gave more importance to what others would think about me. I couldn't bear to choose a career in which I wouldn't earn as much as my friends. I crushed my own dreams and joined the corporate world. However, I was burned out within ten years, and finally realized that the path I had chosen wasn't for me. So then I switched back to the career which I knew would give me the most satisfaction – working with the human mind.

Core beliefs passed on by parents have the power to bind you for the rest of your lives. In some families, parents chain their children with the belief that they have to care for them in their old age. They will remind their children of the many sacrifices they made to raise them. This will keep the children shackled for life in shame and guilt. These children will not be allowed to fly on their own and form their own identities. They will draw their identities from their last names rather than their first names. All their beliefs—be it about romantic relationships, money, career, or spirituality will follow that of their parents. In the culture that I come from, it is very common to have many generations living under one roof. The family includes not just the couple and their kids, but the parents, siblings, grandparents, uncles, aunts, and cousins. It's a patriarchal society where the son lives in the same house as his parents even when he grows up. He starts his own family in the same house, under the watchful eyes of his parents. The son is tied to the family unit and live by its constraints. He is not free to exercise his choices, even in love. He is slated to become the next patriarch, and take care of the parents when they grow old. When I look back at my life, I see my father, brother, and everyone else shackled in these values. However, it became much more apparent to me after I got married, and saw my own husband operating with the same values. I was longing for the romantic love seen in movies and novels, but found that there was no space in real life for that to happen. The integration of the couple was not as important as the integration of the family. There could be no compromise with family pride. Before being husband and wife, we were daughter and son, daughter-in-law and son-in-law. There was no space and time for our relationship to blossom, and because of the lack of a strong bond, many misunderstandings sprung between us. We lost our peace of mind, took wrong financial decisions, and our physical health was impacted, and we lost the intimacy in our relationship. I firmly believe that family beliefs have the power to bind you in an unhealthy way. It stops you from acting in a humane way, and keeps you stuck in stubborn roles.

After living with a set of beliefs for a long time, it is very easy to get blinded to them and their consequences. Instead of mastering our minds, we let our minds rule us. Thus, we're on an auto-pilot mode, and as a result, most of our beliefs are not consciously apparent to us. We're completely dominated by our belief systems. But do you even realize that it's us who created these belief systems in the first place? The good news is that there is always a way to reboot our systems. Our decisions and actions are the tell-tale signs of our beliefs; by assessing them, we can change the harmful beliefs. Now is the time to become the sheriff to YOUR belief structure, instead of your belief structure being the sheriff to you. You can replace all the bricks and stones when they become cracked, weak, inflexible, and when they no longer support your life structure, since you were the one who put them into the structure of your life in the first place. Remember, you can consciously choose new bricks which are flexible, supportive, and rewarding to lead a more joyful and balanced life. It is necessary to take stock of your core beliefs from time to time, and introspect on their impact. I term this as "belief work" which empowers people to replace negative beliefs with positive ones. Once your beliefs are shifted, you behavior/actions will get modified accordingly. The interesting part is that this will open up a new world in your mind which you never knew existed. Our beliefs are interconnected in a tightly knit mesh; a shift in one belief has an impact on all the other beliefs. There are different ways in which our beliefs play up in our lives. See certain examples below:

- *Belief*: **I'm an innocent person.** *My outlook*: People are manipulative. *Effect*: My body language, words, and actions will reflect helplessness and overdependence on others. I will also not be able to take responsibility for the hurt I inflict on others. I will not be able to take charge of my life, and express all the facets of my personality fully. If my family has the same belief, it will be almost impossible for me to see anything else, as I will be constantly validated by them.

• _Belief_: **Anything worthy is acquired with difficultly.** _My outlook_: Challenge motivates me. _Effect_: I will escalate every situation into a challenge. I will be over-competitive with people at work. I will strive for perfection. I will bring challenges into my relationships. I will have to sort out the mess others create for me. Most likely the mess is self-created, so that I can satisfy my need for challenge.

• _Belief_: **No one understands me.** _My outlook_: I was born alone, and I will die alone. Effect: I will feel that no one understands me. I won't be vulnerable, and I will alienate all the people in my life. This will, in turn, further strengthen the feeling of not being understood. This will quickly become a self-fulfilling cycle.

• _Scenario_: You didn't get the promotion you were hoping for. _Thoughts_: **What will people think of me now? How will I show my face to my friend who brags in front of me?** No one understands the struggle I'm going through. My father was such a success, but look at me. _Action_: You might call someone you trust to vent it all out. You might get angry about your life, and take it out on others, leading to road rage, fights with neighbor, arguments with your wife, scolding your children. _Underlying belief_: Money is my identity. People will respect me only when I'm successful. I have to stand up for my family pride. I feel connected to others in pain. It is justified to show anger at others.

I've listed some common beliefs that shape our thought processes. Do you resonate with any of these thoughts, and do any of these occur in your life?

- People will respect me only if I have money.

- Money comes easily and effortlessly.

- People who have money are not humble or grounded.

- I'm born poor.

- I'm alone.

- I don't belong in this world.

- No one understands me.

- Money is success.

- People are mean, don't trust them.

- A penny saved is a penny earned.

- I have to save my family.

- It is everybody else's fault.

- Changing my behavior is impossible.

- I have to be the best or I'll be nothing.

- I need to have authority to gain respect.

- Love doesn't happen to all.

- My life is just a waste.

- Marriage is a challenge.

- Life is not worth it.

- Criticism motivates.

- I belong to a respectable family.

- My kids are my world.

- I'm ugly.

- I'm not worthy of my parent's respect.

- I have to carry my parents' burdens.

- Emotions make us weak.

- Alternative healers are quacks.

- Sufferers are innocent.

- A mother carries pure love.

- Men are evil.

- Women are inferior to men.

- My religion is the true one.

- I'm from a higher social class.

- My sibling is better than me.

- Love isn't real.

- I can't survive without help.

- I have to prove myself to get love.

- I don't deserve money.

If you stay aware then you will see that everything you believe in becomes your life. Our life is totally dominated by the beliefs that we have. Whatever we believe is creating the story that we're experiencing, and these stories are creating our emotions. And, we really want to believe that whatever we believe is the ultimate truth. But this idea is completely false. This is not you. The real and unique you is beyond everything that you know. You haven't even discovered it. What you believe about yourself is not real. This can be tested in the now, if you choose to believe in a different story. You will be surprised how your older beliefs suddenly lose their power over you.

Around the age of sixteen, I was twenty pounds overweight, and believed that "I'm unlovable" and that "love is given only to people with beauty." I would try various diet programs which would make me lose some fat initially. However, soon, the fat would come right back in. It was a hopeless situation. By the time I reached the age of eighteen, my beliefs around love shifted. I started becoming aware of the uniqueness in everyone, and realized that it's our uniqueness that makes us beautiful. I began to appreciate myself for who I was, fat and flabby. With this newfound acceptance, I began caring for myself – not to get acceptance from others, but out of love for myself. Magically, my fat began disappearing on its own. What had looked impossible earlier turned into reality without even trying. It was self-acceptance that helped me finally come out of the feeling that "I wasn't good enough".

In today's time, we can learn about the concept of beliefs through internet, books, and various other sources. But many of us make excuses by waiting for others to make the first move to initiate change, or for the opportunity to present itself. They may say, "I'm changing but others are not," and that pulls them back to their old patterns. We come up with excuse after excuse after excuse so that we don't have to ask ourselves this one question: "Am I willing to put in what it takes, time, effort, and consistent practice, to change my belief structure, irrespective of whether others are changing or not, whether situations present themselves or not, whether our luck changes or not?"

The following exercise will uncover a lot about you and your core beliefs, and will help you change them for a better life.

Step 1: For the list of topics given below, write down what thoughts come to you. For helping you through this exercise, I'm listing a few examples.

<u>Examples</u>:

	How do you deal with your own emotions?	How do you perceive/act with others when they exhibit the following emotions?
Anger	I try to keep quiet, withdraw, and suppress it most of the times.	How bad of them to yell at others! I don't want to associate with them.
Needs (emotional, physical, mental)	I hint rather than ask directly, but sometimes get passive aggressive when the other person can't guess what I want.	I feel they are so mean and needy to ask for it openly. They are so inconsiderate about other's needs.
Approval/Rejection	I feel shame when rejected even during a small inconsequential conversation. And, the slightest of approval tells me that I'm worthy and I'm going in the right direction.	How flimsy of him to seek approval, and their rejection makes me feel empathy towards them.

Use the table below to record your responses

	How do you deal with your own emotions?	How do you perceive/act with others when they exhibit the following emotions?
Anger		
Needs (emotional, physical, mental)		
Approval/ Rejection		
Self-care		

Failures		
Body Image		
Financial status / Spending habits		
Dependence / Trust		
Blame		
Loss of loved ones		
Stress management style		
Taking risks		
Creativity		
Boundaries		
Shame		
Negative/ Positive outlook in life		
Romance		
Partnership with significant other		
Seek help		

Write down what these statements mean to you.

- How important is it for you to get your parent's approval on your life decisions? How is it working out in your life?

- How should you behave in a family? Around elders and youngsters?

- What constitutes family life for you? How should it look like?

- What according to you is good social behavior with extended family and society? How much of that do you actually exhibit?

- What is the role of a man in a family?

- What is the role of a woman in a family?

- Do you believe that elders are wise and that their advice needs to be respected/followed?

- Is it okay to keep secrets with your parents?

- Is it okay to keep secrets with your spouse?

- Is it important to help others?

- What does recreation/relaxation look like in your life?

- How do you behave with people of a lower socio-economic status?

- How do you behave with people of a higher socio-economic status?

- Do you feel that your actions are role modelled on those of your parents?

- What do you like and dislike about yourself? How do you manage being:

  → Alone?

  → With strangers?

  → With friends?

  → With family?

- How do you make friends?

- How do you deal with children?

- How do you manage your health or illness?

Look at each of your responses above, and think how old these beliefs are. More likely than not all these beliefs will have their root in your childhood. Either you would have taken your parents as your role models, or you're trying to overcompensate for the emptiness you felt as a child.

Step 2: Uncover your core beliefs using the downward arrow technique.

- From your responses above, pick out some common themes/thoughts that you see running through all your answers.

- Ask yourself what that thought tells about you. Think about it in terms of you as a person. Your answer can be something like, "I'm afraid of failure," or "I'm too scared of getting embarrassed."

- Repeat the process to question yourself, and uncover yet another layer of thought. Your underlying thought could look like: "I'm not good enough," or "I'm weak."

- Continue this process until you come to terms with your core beliefs.

Step 3: Choose a specific core belief which is unpowerful, and is not working out in your life. Write down a new powerful belief you wish to adopt. Try and understand what catastrophes might happen if you were to act against your core belief. Some examples are provided below. In the blank rows, you can write your rules and the predicted catastrophes.

Rule sustaining your belief	Catastrophic prediction
Keep the peace.	The other person will get angrier. It will be my fault. The relationship will end
Don't express needs directly..	I will be rejected. It will be embarrassing if I am told that my needs are unimportant.
Don't disagree.	I will be wrong. Everyone will know I'm stupid.
Don't make decisions or take actions	I will do the wrong thing or make matters worse.

You've acknowledged the fears – the catastrophes – that these rules are designed to avoid.

Step 4: The next stage is to pick up a rule from the list above that you would like to change. This step is designed to make you feel confident while making a new rule. It will help you form a new belief and change for the better.

Rehearsing is an important step before the situation occurs. For me, visualizing is an effective tool. If it's something involving communication, for example, practice it beforehand either with another person or alone in front of a mirror. You can even record a video of yourself while you're practicing. Then examine your voice and posture to ensure you've got it right. Remember, if there is an undesirable outcome, it is nothing to worry about. Create a step-by-step plan for solving the problem, and immediately script your new behavior.

Congratulations, you have created new responses. These new rules will help you make a better life, shake off the old beliefs, and develop new desired ones.

Old rules	New responses
Keep the peace.	I can cope with conflict.
Don't express needs directly.	My needs are as important as anyone else's.
Don't disagree.	I want to be the kind of person who stands up for their beliefs.
Don't express anger.	I can solve problems by expressing my anger in respectful ways.
Don't make decisions or take actions.	I have good judgment. I can solve problems.

CHAPTER 13

TECHNOLOGY

"The difference between technology and slavery is that slaves are fully aware that they are not free."

— Nassim Nicholas Taleb

The impact of technology on human relationships has claimed the attention of many theorists. It is a known fact that social connections are the basis of the human condition. We live and thrive on the basis of our secure bonding with others around us. Technology has thrown open many new electronic platforms for collaborating with others. The promise of a smaller world, and the closer relationships with these new tools are very enticing. Technology has revolutionized our world, and has made all the information in the world come literally to our finger tips, and deliver many conveniences like online shopping. The world has become one big platform. Trade and commerce have grown exponentially around the world. Businesses are now able to advertise and deliver products and services with ease. Collaboration among people has grown tremendously to deliver new inventions and products. We're all aware about the positive impact of technology, and it will take reams of pages to described how it has enhanced our lives. However, the overuse of technology, especially social media, which has now become our primary means of communication these days is the demon lurking within the shadows. I fear there will come a day when the news of a relative's demise will be shared on social media, and we will offer our condolences through thumbs-down and sad emojis. The question is not why these platforms exist, but why we're unable to find the right balance while using them. So, the intent of this chapter is to highlight how the overuse of technology is harming us.

When I was in college, I used to pay by the minute to use internet. In those days, we used the internet to collect information while doing a project. Because I was paying by the minute, I would limit my internet usage to essential work only. I would spend the rest of my time interacting with friends, reading books, going for walks, or going for art classes. Those days we only had one landline phone at home for the whole family to use. Telephone calls were expensive, and so our conversations were also limited and to the point. We had the ten-digit phone numbers of at least ten-fifteen people on the tip of our tongues. It was a nice feeling to make and receive phone calls so that we could wish each other on important occasions. Interactions were more personal and heartfelt. The world was still functioning well; information was still getting disseminated, and people were still employed. That time felt holistic, joyful, and yet connected.

Cut to the present. Nowadays we jump out of our beds to check our phones, take our phones to the bathroom, talk on the phone while driving, keep checking our social media pages for updates, check our phones while eating lunch, fiddle with our phones at the traffic signal, watch TV while eating food, listen to music while working out, watch videos on the phone before going to bed, etc. For more entertainment, we go out for movies. When we go out with our families for dinner, all of us are busy looking at our phones. We sleep and get up with our phones instead of our partners. These days we know more about our favorite vlogger than about our spouse and kids. We may be in a room full of people, but we'll still be more interested in our phones.

All aspects of our lives are suffering because of this overindulgence in our smartphones. It has now become an extension of our bodies which we can't live without. We're not able to see the link between the dysfunction in our lives and the overuse of gadgets.

- Interacting with technology has become a compulsive behavior that is similar to substance abuse. This is escapist behavior to avoid dealing with our own emotions. We have found a constant noise which helps us block the voice inside our heads. This is an easy way to distract yourself and avoid introspecting about things which really matter. In the families of today, it is common to see that the family members are shut off to each other's emotions. They are busy in their fast-paced digital worlds, and are far removed from reality. One of the main causes of people feeling alone and empty is the fact that our own family members lack the emotional context to understand our problems. We're more interested in connecting with people whom we don't live with physically, and end up ignoring those who are around us. Next time notice if you're habitually checking your phone every five-ten minutes even if there is no notification.

- Relationship breakdown - Lack of intimacy, absolute disconnection with the partner, living like strangers are all common occurrences in relationships now, thanks to the advent of smartphones. Even when we're together we like to watch TV and go for movies. When the couple goes out shopping, the person waiting outside the trial room is on the phone, and any free moment in between is consumed by the phone. This lack of awareness about each other's moods and emotions has resulted in failed marriages. The anxiety we feel when our phone's battery is running out is higher than what we feel when the battery of our relationships start running out. I remember a time when I was saying something very important to my husband. In the middle of the discussion, he started responding to someone's messages. This made me feel as if he didn't think what I had to say was important. When I confronted him about this, he said, "Is it not normal to respond to someone's message when you see a notification?" This was not the only time. Even in date nights he would be preoccupied with the daily news or with emails, and we wouldn't be able to have any healthy conversations. We were mentally separating from each other, and I was feeling very anxious. Until he understood my complaints and rectified his behavior, I used to feel as if his phone was his real wife. I'm sure I'm not the exception, and most of us feel disconnected with our loved ones because of gadgets.

- We have very superficial relationships with our children nowadays. We're so consumed by our own distractions that we're not able to meet the emotional needs of our children. Boundaries between children and parents have been blurred by the oversharing of information through social media.

• Our senses are constantly active and are bombarded with information left, right, and center. We don't realize that everything we see and hear on social media has a context, and if we fail to realize this context correctly then it creates unnecessary excitation in our minds. And, we get addicted to this excitation. We keep going back to it until we're mentally spent and exhausted. We live in a zombieland, hypnotized by our make-belief digital worlds, walking, eating, and resting with our heads bent and eyes fixated on our smartphones. Our emotions are numbed as if we have checked out from our own bodies. We develop behavioral and sleep disorders. We're now living for the likes and dislikes that we get on social media for our posts. That is our achievement now. Can you imagine what will happen if someone kidnapped your phone for a week? I think we would be ready to kill for our true love. Doesn't it seem like the script of the next blockbuster movie?

• Social media has become a validation platform where everyone is flaunting made-up images about their lives. We dress up and plaster ourselves with makeup to click a picture which we can then post on Instagram. The moment we check into a new place, the update has to go up on Facebook. We talk on Snapchat or make a TikTok video at any given free time. Self-worth is now derived from the number of likes and comments that our posts generate. We know too much about each other, which restaurant we're at, where we went for our last vacation, our latest fitness regime, our promotion at work, our new car, or the interior décor of our home. These images from our lives just show a part of the story, but not the whole reality. We show people the happy bits while hiding the sadness. And, this raises the bar of superficiality. We all compete with each other to show off our perfect lives. We're trying to outdo each other in all aspects. And, in trying to do so, the moments we cherish with our partners, families, or by ourselves have lost the meaning that they once carried, because every possible moment is now meant to be captured on camera and shared with the virtual world. We now habitually share each and everything, however personal it maybe, with complete strangers. We have become hyper-connected, and as a result, we're getting disconnected from ourselves and from others.

- We underestimate the different kinds of influences we have from social media. When we see our favorite actors endorse some products it makes us want to have those products. We assume that if we also flaunt those same products on social media it will get us followers and subscribers. I remember drooling over the images of some furniture on social media, and I didn't even think about whether I needed them, or if they even matched my home décor. I just wanted them because I was enamored by their statement and luxury. Definitely I'm not the only one who behaves like this from time to time. Each of us is trying to up our living standard to keep up with others. In our free time, we check out the images of the expensive homes, cars, and vacations that our friends and relatives post. We want what others have to keep up with the Joneses, and would rather not meet others until we're able to match their standards. These days, relationships and friendships mean nothing as compared to the need to show off.

- A lot of content on the internet promotes bullying and body shaming. From standup comedies to independent videos to social media posts, these platforms are filled with vicious people who troll others mercilessly. These anonymous internet trolls have no moral barriers, and they say hurtful things about content creators to insult and incite. Things which were once thought of as culturally inappropriate have come out into the open and into our living rooms. Victims of cyberbullying are humiliated and shamed in front of the entire world. Our concept of fitness, beauty, health, success, happiness has become completely distorted, thanks to all the edited photos doing the rounds on the internet. This has led to an increased rate of depression all over the world.

- A research has revealed that more that 95% of us use technology in the hour before going to bed. This makes it tougher for us to fall asleep. Overuse of technology has become the leading cause of poor sleep which has severe consequences like weight gain, depression, anxiety, and ADD (Attention Deficit Disorder). Those who are incapable of using technology are also prone to anxiety because a lot of work in the world is now done solely through technological means. But the people who are compulsively overusing technology are more prone to anxiety than those who don't use it at all. This concludes that we all need to know how to use technology, but we shouldn't submit to it like slaves.

- We have lost the ability to sit and focus. With so many distractions around us these days, we have become habitual multi-taskers. We think we're getting a lot done, however with an unfocused mind, we're not being as effective as we think. On the other hand, our abilities to comprehend, understand, and then act has reduced. Imagine that you're trying to complete an urgent task on your laptop, but you're being constantly bombarded with emails, IMs, text messages, calls, notifications, etc. It will be impossible for you to concentrate on the task at hand. In today's workplaces, we have too many tools that facilitate collaboration. Instead of increasing productivity, they become the main cause for distraction and poor output. The virtuous acts of being calm, composed, and attentive, which were once considered important, have now become impossible states to attain. We have become very fidgety, distracted, forgetful, anxious, irritable, frustrated, and short-tempered.

- Children are being overexposed to technology since their infancy now. A one-year-old these days has a tablet that she can interact with all day. Parents use this as a tool to keep their toddlers engaged so that they don't bother them. It's easy for children to get exposed to mature content online, and be negatively influenced by it. Children take online personalities as their role models, and may get hooked to dangerous addictions that their idols might also have. I recently saw that some teenagers killed innocent animals, and shamelessly posted a picture of themselves with the dead bodies on social media as if they had just won a trophy. This was supposedly construed as their rite of passage. Other children can easily get influenced by such posts, and start emulating such grotesque behavior. They can also become victims of online predators, or dangerous online games. There was an online game called Blue Whale which made children inflict increasing degrees of torture on themselves, ending in eventual suicide. A study has confirmed that interaction with technology makes children mature much faster than before. The rate of childhood obesity has also increased because children are now stuck with their gadgets all day, and they don't go out to play anymore.

Addictions don't necessarily mean substance abuse. A fixation on any one thing or activity is a kind of addiction too, where our minds constantly desire instant gratification from that particular object or task. The good news is that no matter how badly you're addicted, you can always have a complete remission. It's time to hit the reset button in order to achieve the union of mind and body. We need to create a healthy balance by staying in the grey area and not swinging to either extremes of not using technology at all or using it excessively. The exercise given below will give you a good start, but you'll need to be truthful in answering

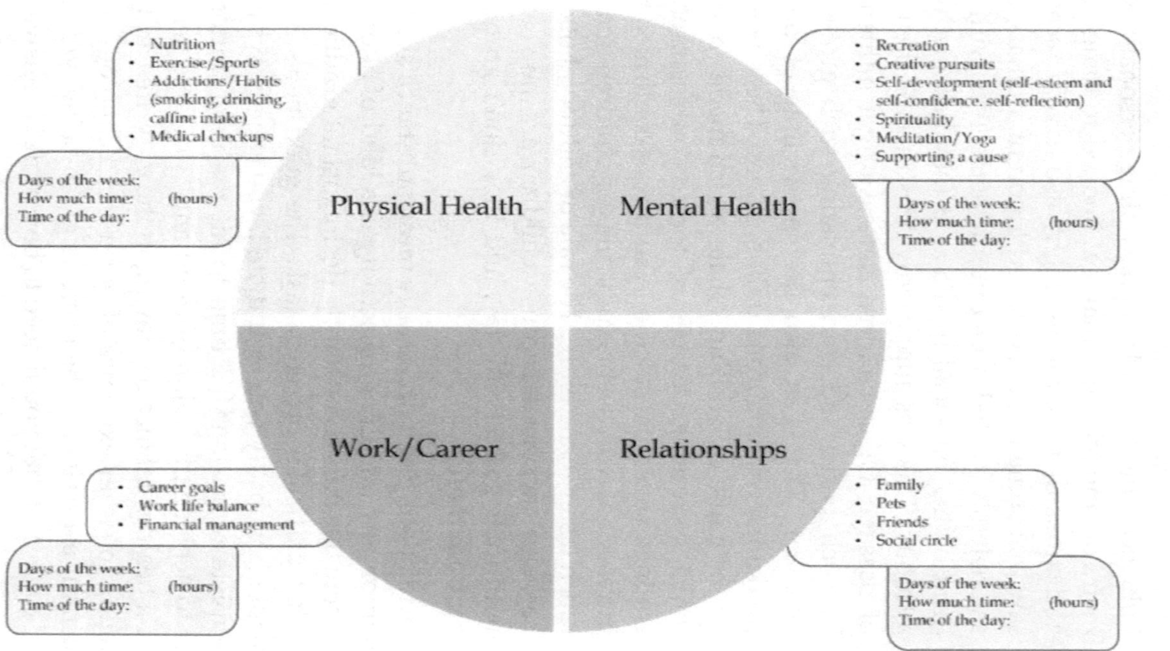
Physical Health
Nutrition
Exercise/Sports
Addictions/Habits (smoking, drinking, caffine intake)
Medical checkups
Days of the week:
How much time: (hours)
Time of the day:

Mental Health
Recreation
Creative pursuits
Self-development (self-esteem and self-confidence, self-reflection)
Spirituality
Meditation/Yoga
Supporting a cause
Days of the week:
How much time: (hours)
Time of the day:

Work/Career
Career goals
Work life balance
Financial management
Days of the week:
How much time: (hours)
Time of the day:

Relationships
Family
Pets
Friends
Social circle
Days of the week:
How much time: (hours)
Time of the day:

these questions.

1. **Goal Setting:** The picture given below shows the most prominent aspects of life. A healthy life can only come about when all these facets are in order. Decide how much time you wish to allocate to each of these areas in your life, and at what time of the day.

2. More likely than not you will be surprised to see how much valuable time you spend on your devices, time which you could have used to do useful things. You can get an accurate idea of the time you spend on social media through some apps that can be downloaded from the internet.

3. Once you have filled your day with goals that are important to you, think about how much time you're left with to spare for technology or social media.

4. You may realize that you can free up a significant amount of time by cutting down the time you spend on technological distractions. Now think about the important activity that you have been postponing for days because you thought you didn't have enough time. You can reorganize your daily schedule now, and fit in important tasks.

5. Here are some tools that you can use to ensure that you stay on track.

    a. *Keep a planner, either physical or electronic.* Everyone has more than enough things to be done in their lives. However, only the things that are salient, or demand our immediate attention, are the ones which get done. It's easy to pick up the smartphone and forget about other things if they are not urgent. But when we plan things in advance, we can ensure that things get done at the right time and with more efficiency.

b. _A fun way to get household chores_ done is to put up a list of tasks on the refrigerator, and assign each task to individual members in the family. This fosters team spirit in the family while ensuring that things get done on time.

c. _Impose a curfew time on technology_ when you spend time with your family, say, 6-9 p.m. After work when you wish to engage with your children (6-8 p.m.) and partner (8-9 p.m.), it is important to stay away from your phone. Keep your phone tucked away when you're with your family. With all the free time available now, it becomes possible to connect with your dear ones. Pay attention to their verbal and non-verbal cues. The more inquisitive and curious you can remain with yourself and your family members, the deeper, healthier, and more secure relationships you will develop. Listen actively and ask questions which can give you an insight into the thought processes of your family members like "What does it mean to you?" or "What do you think about this?" or "What's important about this?" or "What are the challenges you're facing?"

d. Plan for some "_me time_" in your day. It could be a morning walk, exercising, or reading a book before going to bed. Spend time with your thoughts, and free yourself from distractions. This helps you introspect and connect with yourself. Without this, it is easy to slip into a robotic life where you forget to think about what really matters.

e. _Switch off the app notifications on your phone._ Why do we need to be notified about petty news, spam messages, or social media updates every second? This prevents you from giving undivided attention to the task at hand. Check your phone for important messages only during designated times.

f. _Don't take your phone to your bedroom._ The bedroom is a sacred space for the couple, and it should not be violated. The time you spend in the bedroom should be full of intimacy and free from distractions. It's not healthy to lie in your bed and stare at the TV screen for hours. Use a separate alarm clock rather than the alarm on your phone. Give yourself thirty to forty-five minutes in bed before you go to sleep and after you wake up.

g. _Know how to say "no" to temptations and instant gratifications._ These days every website uses your browsing history to send you personalized suggestions, leaving you more susceptible to bite the bait. We don't even realize how many months and years of our lives get wasted in mindless browsing and shopping on the internet. It's time to say "no", and keep your priority list at hand.

h. Introspect and write down what is your ideal

image of beauty, fitness, social status, career, job profile, financial status, homes, brands, cars, vacations, parties, etc. Can you now notice how it is being influenced by images that you've seen on TV or on social media? It's time we stop making perfectionism a norm, and stop deriving our sense of self-worth from the attainment of these impossible goals. Rather than drawing your identity through external validation from others on social media, affirm strongly over and over again: "My self-worth is dependent on how I treat myself, and not on what others say."

EPILOGUE

I hope you enjoyed reading this book and were able to derive some value out of it. If you could affect an iota of change in your life because of this book, I would consider it as a personal success. I know it's not easy because old habits die hard. This is also true for habits stemming from drama, judgment, blame, anger, negative thinking, shame, etc. If you were able to apply the principles of this book in some areas of your life and create a positive change for yourself, you'll be in for a treat. As you keep chipping away at your old patterns using your newfound insights, you will realize that a whole world is opening up for you. The more you practice, the better will you get at finding old patterns and replacing them with those that will help you create a powerful future, not just for yourself, but also for those around you. The more effort you put into it, the greater will be the rewards.

I've been trying and testing these principles in my life for many years now. It helped me choose the right partner and weather many a storm in my life. If the foundation is strong, the building survives, largely intact, even in the worst conditions. I've found that to be true even for life in general. If your guiding principles are strongly rooted, you remain largely unshaken, even in the most turbulent of times. Another effect of living life with clarity is that people either get "chained or changed". I find that all relationships are like seesaws; all of us are constantly balancing each other. If you change your position, and stand your ground, the other people will have to shift to a complementary position and will "be chained to you". Or they will leave you for good if they are not able to keep up: "changed or replaced". Though it may sound so, it is not a bad outcome at all. You don't have to carry everyone with you as you move ahead in your life. Sometimes, it's better to part ways when the journey with them is over and you encounter a fork in the road of life. You were meant for different destinations; don't fret about it, it's only natural.

A life of clarity is a life of power. Power doesn't mean dominance, rather it means having the tools to create and cause a desirable change. Unhindered by the unwanted noises in your life, your power to create and change will astound you. However, there isn't any shortcut–achieving this power requires effort, real effort.

"The secret of change is to focus all your energy, not on fighting the old, but building the new." – Socrates